Reader's Digest
Wild**Britain**

ANIMALS

PUBLISHED BY
THE READER'S DIGEST ASSOCIATION LIMITED
LONDON ■ NEW YORK ■ SYDNEY ■ MONTREAL

CONTENTS

ANIMALS

FIELDCRAFT

UNDERSTANDING ANIMALS

THIS BOOK COVERS all vertebrate (backboned) animals, apart from birds, that live wild on land in Britain. It includes all four-legged animals and also snakes and the slow-worm – limbless vertebrates – as well as seals, which spend part of their lives on land and part in water. It does not include fish and whales – vertebrates which live entirely in water – nor does it cover invertebrate land animals such as slugs, snails, worms and woodlice, which do not have bony skeletons.

The land animals described in this book belong to one or other of three major groups: amphibians, reptiles or mammals. Each has evolved different ways of using energy and reproducing its kind.

Amphibians are animals such as frogs, which have soft, moist skins and can breathe air on land or absorb oxygen through the skin when under water. They live in damp places on land, taking wholly to the water for a while in spring to breed. They lay eggs that hatch into tadpoles, which live and grow entirely in the water for the first few weeks of life until they are transformed into tiny adults ready for life on land.

Reptiles are animals such as snakes, which have dry, scaly skins. They have lungs and breathe air, and their waterproof skins enable them to live in dry places. Some lay eggs and others give birth to live young.

Both amphibians and reptiles are 'cold blooded', which means their body temperatures vary according to those of their surroundings. They are fully active only when outside warmth raises their body temperature to a high enough level, generally about 25-32°C. Muscle, nerve and digestive action increase at higher temperatures, and all animals must achieve a certain body temperature before they can be fully active.

Mammals are 'warm blooded', with body temperatures normally higher than those of their surroundings – usually 32-40°C. This enables them to be active at any time. They have hairy or furry bodies and feed their young on milk.

Plant-eating animals are known as herbivores. Some, such as deer, are totally herbivorous; others will occasionally take different food – grey squirrels, for instance, will take birds' eggs. Animals that feed almost entirely on flesh are described as carnivores, and animals that feed on both plants and flesh are omnivores. Animals that eat mainly insects are called insectivores.

Animal classification

The smallest natural group to which an animal belongs is called the species. Animals of the same species are able to interbreed and produce fertile offspring. Those of different species do not normally do so.

Although an animal's common name usually indicates its species – weasel, for example – names can vary from place to place, so animals are given a scientific name based on Latin or Greek. The weasel's scientific name is *Mustela nivalis*, of which *nivalis* is the species name and *Mustela* the genus name – a name shared by other closely related animals of a different species. So the related stoat is *Mustela erminea*.

When more than one genus closely resembles another, they are grouped to form a family. The stoat and weasel, for example, belong to the Family Mustelidae. Families are also grouped into related orders. The mustelids belong to the order Carnivora – flesh-eating animals.

How to use this book

The main part of this book features more than 70 wild land animals of Britain, species by species. The wild species are divided into three major groups – mammals, amphibians and reptiles. The mammals are further grouped mainly according to their classification orders. An identification key appears on pages 26-31, and this will direct you to the pages for the group.

Recognition characteristics are given for each species, and also their habits, lifespan and a guide to habitat – where the animal normally lives. These characteristics include a guide to the animal's size; where the male and female are appreciably different in size, this is stated.

The life expectancy given for any animal is only an indication of how long it might live in reasonable conditions. It is not a true average lifespan for the species. Many wild animals die not long after birth, but the survivors may live for a number of years.

As many animals are active only after dark, tell-tale signs of their presence, such as tracks and food remains, are more often seen than the animals themselves. The 'Fieldcraft' section (pages 232-51) gives some idea of the signs to look for in various types of country. Throughout the book there are also a number of features showing how the lifestyle of certain animals is related to their surroundings.

To help you to understand how an animal's observed behaviour is linked to its body structure and lifestyle, pages 8-25 outline some of the reasons why animals feed, breed and behave in different ways.

Using the maps

Distribution maps are given for each of the wild species in the book. On each map, the area of the country coloured in maroon is where you may find the species, which is also described in the caption below.

SKIN

AN ANIMAL'S SKIN is adapted to its needs and its way of life. Typically, mammals have an insulating covering of fur – fine, closely packed hairs – because their body heat is generated internally and they need to prevent its loss. They need a thick coat to keep them warm in winter and a thinner coat in summer, so they moult to change the coat once or twice a year. Moulting is triggered by seasonal changes in day length and temperature, and controlled by hormones in the blood.

Reptiles and amphibians such as snakes and frogs absorb heat from their surroundings. A furry skin would impede the process, so reptiles have thin skin protected by thin scales, and amphibians have bare skin.

Waterproof skin
Reptiles have a fully waterproof skin, so can live in both wet and dry places without losing precious body moisture. The skin is shed periodically, the dull, worn outer surface being scraped off in one piece or several, revealing bright new colours.

Otter

Waterproof fur
Mammals such as the mink and the otter that spend a lot of time in the water are in particular danger of losing body heat. To avoid this they have a furry coat, in two layers. The under layer consists of fine hairs that trap air against the skin, giving insulation and warmth. A top layer of longer hairs provides a sleek and streamlined shape, and keeps the underfur dry.

Common frog

Skin that aids breathing
A frog's skin has glands that keep it moist so that it can absorb oxygen from the air, and so serves as a kind of lung. This limits frogs to living in wet or damp places. Frogs can also live under water, the skin acting as a kind of gill.

Grass snake

Common shrew

A new coat twice a year
Shrews moult twice a year. The short summer coat is shed in October, starting at the rump and moving forwards. It is replaced by longer winter fur. This is moulted in spring, starting at the head, and replaced by shorter fur for the warmer months. Many rodents also moult twice a year.

Spiky hairs for protection

A hedgehog's spines are hairs modified to perform a protective role. They can be made to point in any direction, forming a protective jacket like barbed wire that few predators will breach. Spines cannot be moulted all at once or they lose their value. They are lost and re-grown one at a time over long periods.

Stoat

A coat that changes colour

Stoats and mountain hares change their coats in winter, and many go white at the same time, possibly triggered by sudden cold. The change of colour may act as camouflage in snowy surroundings and provide better heat conservation, as white radiates less energy.

A new summer coat

Foxes moult once a year, in early summer. Their thick winter coat is replaced by a shorter one that makes them look slimmer and longer-legged. As cold weather begins in autumn, more hairs grow and thicken the coat. As the density increases the hairs cannot all lay flat, and stand out from the skin, giving the fox a robust, stocky appearance.

Fat layers for warmth

Seals live in the water but do not have a double-layered coat like mink or otters, being kept warm instead by thick layers of fat beneath the skin. Insulating underfur might spoil their streamlined shape, and when diving deep its effect would be reduced as the air was squeezed out. Grey seals and common seals have short, stiff guard hairs that protect the skin from abrasion by rocks and sand.

Grey seal

Specially developed underfur

Domestic sheep have been specially bred to develop exaggerated curly underfur, which now forms their whole coat. It is this 'wool' that is spun into yarn or pressed into felt. Long, straight guard hairs are not wanted, as they cannot be linked up to form threads or felt, and would weaken the material.

STRUCTURE

ALTHOUGH MANY of Britain's mammals, reptiles and amphibians look very different from each other, they have the same basic bone structure. All have evolved over millions of years from the same ancestors, so are variations on the same theme. The rabbit skeleton on page 249 shows the standard pattern, except that snakes and slow-worms have no leg bones. In all four-limbed animals, the forelimb joints compare with those of the human arm, and the hindlimb joints with those of the human leg. See below for the similarities in forelimb bones for some animals that differ greatly in size and shape.

Just as the skeletons of land animals are similar, so too are the layouts of their muscles, their digestive systems, and their arrangements for breathing. But mammals have more highly developed and efficient blood-circulation systems than reptiles and amphibians, which gives them the ability to be much more active.

Typical foreleg bones
The bones in a badger's foreleg are typical of many land animals. It has a large shoulder blade, a single upper bone and twin bones in the lower leg. Small bones form the wrist, and each of the five toes has four bones, the end one with a horny claw attached.

Daubenton's bat

Forelimbs as wings
In a bat's forelimb, the four digits, or fingers, are enormously extended to support the wing membrane between them. The fifth digit, or thumb, is not linked to the membrane and has a large claw used by the bat to hang or pull itself along.

Forelimbs as flippers
Most of the forelimb of a seal is buried in its body, but it still has the standard bone pattern. The five toes, each with a long claw, are joined closely to form a flipper. This is used to steer in the water, but not for walking on land.

Common seal

Forelegs with extra power
A digging animal such as a mole needs powerful muscles, anchored to prominent projections on bones. The relative sizes of bones are adapted to give extra leverage. A mole's upper foreleg bone is enormous, and it has a front foot that looks rather like a huge hand but is not very flexible.

Goat

Long and short necks

All mammals have seven bones in the neck, whether it is long (as in a goat, deer or horse), short (as in a vole or seal) or apparently non-existent (as in a mole).

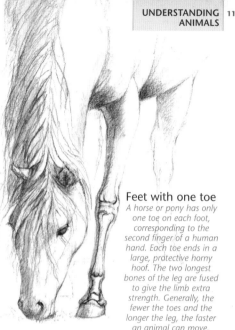

Feet with one toe

A horse or pony has only one toe on each foot, corresponding to the second finger of a human hand. Each toe ends in a large, protective horny hoof. The two longest bones of the leg are fused to give the limb extra strength. Generally, the fewer the toes and the longer the leg, the faster an animal can move.

Feet with two toes

Sheep – like cows, pigs, goats and deer – have two toes on each foot ending in a cloven hoof. The remnants of two more toes appear as dew claws higher up the leg. There is no trace of a big toe. As with horses, the two longest bones of the leg are fused to give extra strength.

Tails that are not obvious

Even animals that apparently have no tail still have the bones that would otherwise form it. In frogs and toads the bones are joined as a single rod that lies within the pelvis. Snakes have quite short tails – about a third or less of their length.

Legs that spread sideways

A lizard's foreleg has the same bone pattern as a badger's, but its legs are spread sideways rather than held downwards. Newts are like lizards in posture but do not need such robust bones as they spend a lot of time buoyed up in water.

Common lizard

Common frog

BEHAVIOUR AND BODY STRUCTURE

AN ANIMAL'S BEHAVIOUR is linked to its body structure. Some animals have evolved for a certain way of life, which then limits what they can do. Some (known as fossorial) are built for digging burrows. Moles dig well but cannot climb. Squirrels are arboreal (built for living in trees); they climb well but cannot dig burrows and swim poorly. Animals that run fast (cursorial), such as deer, cannot climb trees or use their limbs with the skill of a squirrel.

Some animals – 'Jacks of all trades' – have evolved a less specialised structure that allows them to do all sorts of things moderately well. Rats, for example, can climb, burrow, swim and run fast – not as well as the specialists, but in a way that lets them adapt to any environment, whether indoors, in trees, in burrows or in water.

Most swimming animals push with their feet to force a way through water. This is made easier by webbing between the toes, to provide a larger surface that can 'grip' the water. The water shrew does this with a row of bristles on each of its hind toes, but fully aquatic animals such as the otter have all four feet webbed, and are powerful swimmers. Frogs have fully webbed hind feet, and are better swimmers than toads, which have only partial webbing on the hind feet.

Grooming with the tongue
Cats comb their fur with the tongue because their claws, which are sharp and curved for seizing prey, are not suitable for combing. When not in use, the claws are drawn back over the toes so they do not become blunted. Deer and other hoofed mammals also groom themselves mainly by licking.

Claws for grooming
Like many other mammals, a water vole uses the claws on its forefeet as a comb to groom its fur. Mammals that spend a lot of time in the water groom often because their bodies are less well protected against cold and water if their fur is matted.

Limbs for fast movement
Horses, deer and most other hoofed mammals have developed long, strong limbs so they can run fast and jump well to escape predators. Their feet are strong but light, having only one or two toes, but cannot be used to hold food; the lower leg can be bent only one way, not twisted round.

A tail as an extra limb

A harvest mouse uses the end of its tail to grip twigs and stems as it climbs among them. Its grip is strong enough to support its own weight, so the mouse can stretch to get at food otherwise out of reach.

Tails that flash a warning

A rabbit's bobbing white tail as it runs from danger gives a warning to other rabbits. Muntjac deer show the white underside of the tail when alarmed, and roe and sika deer fluff out their light-coloured rump hairs.

Hind legs for springing away

Frogs, like rabbits, hares and wallabies, have large, powerful hind legs that help them to spring away fast from a standing start. As their front legs are much smaller, they cannot easily walk on all fours but move in characteristic hops and bounds.

Tails that aid balance

Although a black rat cannot grip with its tail like a harvest mouse, it loops and swings its tail to assist balance. This enables it to run fast up or down or along narrow surfaces such as ropes. Brown rats and some mice use their tails in the same way.

Tails for brushing away flies

Horses and ponies can flick their long tails in all directions to brush away irritating flies. Their ability to scratch using their legs and hoofs is very limited.

TEETH

ALL BRITAIN'S LAND ANIMALS have teeth, though those of amphibians such as frogs are tiny. The teeth of mammals are divided into specialist groups – incisors at the front of the mouth for biting, premolars and molars (or cheek teeth) at the back for chewing and grinding, and sharp canines for seizing prey.

This tooth pattern is often modified for a particular diet. Flesh-eaters (carnivores), for example, need sharp canines for seizing and stabbing prey, but plant-eaters (herbivores) usually have no canines because they do not need to seize prey. Plant-eaters tend to have broad teeth, ridged like files, to shred and grind plants to extract all the nourishment.

Carnivorous mammals, notably badgers, that eat plant food as well as flesh are omnivores. Their teeth are broader and better adapted for crushing and grinding than those of mammals that are more strictly carnivorous. Pigs are omnivores and have well-developed canines.

Carnivores, omnivores and insectivores have teeth in a continuous row along the jaw. Herbivores and rodents (gnawing animals such as mice) have a long gap between the incisors and cheek teeth.

Teeth that grow constantly

Squirrels, like all rodents, have big incisors that grow constantly but are kept in trim by gnawing hard food such as nuts. Unless rodents gnaw frequently, their front teeth may grow too long and develop into a grotesque arc.

Chewing the cud

Plant food is hard to digest, so sheep, goats and deer have a specially adapted, multi-chambered stomach. Food is briefly chewed and then swallowed into the first chamber, where it is partly digested. Later, when the animal is resting, wads of food, or cuds, are returned to the mouth for further chewing. Then they are swallowed into a different part of the stomach for complete digestion. Sheep have only a pad at the front of the upper jaw, and small, narrow muzzles that allow them to nibble short grass.

Red squirrel

Teeth for chewing bones

Dogs, foxes and other carnivores turn their heads sideways and use their molars to bite off tough pieces of food or chew a bone. Compared with those of rodents, their incisors are small and weak.

Teeth for seizing prey

As with all flesh-eating animals, a fox has large canines between its incisors and molars. The canines enable it to seize and stab prey and inflict a serious or fatal wound before the victim can escape. Bats are carnivorous and have the same tooth pattern. They need to seize and stab active and relatively large insects.

Grazers that can bite

Horses and ponies can crop grass much closer than cattle, and eat coarser vegetation. This is because they have incisors on both their upper and lower jaws, so can bite their food instead of plucking it. Horses do not chew the cud, so plant material is not thoroughly broken down and may be recognisable in their droppings.

Teeth for eating small prey

Hedgehogs, moles and shrews have lower-jaw incisors that point forwards at an angle. They are effective for picking up small prey such as woodlice, which are crushed on the sharply pointed molars.

Teeth that inject poison

An adder bites its prey with poison fangs. They are hollow teeth which act rather like hypodermic needles and inject poison from glands in the upper jaw into the victim. As snakes swallow their prey whole, they do not need teeth for chewing. They have tiny, sharp, backward-sloping teeth that prevent their prey escaping.

Plant-eaters that feed on leaves

Deer are natural browsers – they feed on the leaves and shoots of trees – but may also graze, especially in parks when they have eaten all the leaves they can reach. As with sheep, they have a tough pad at the front of the upper jaw and incisors on the lower jaw only.

SEEING

AN ANIMAL'S EYES do not see the world in exactly the same way as a human's eyes. Humans can perceive distinct colours, but animals cannot normally see colour to the same extent. Animals that are active by day, such as squirrels, are more likely to see colours. But most land animals are active mainly at night, when they see not in colour but in shades of light and dark. Their eyes are much more sensitive than human eyes and can work at low light levels. On a really dark night, animals can see at least as well as humans do in bright moonlight but no animal can see in total darkness.

Many nocturnal animals, such as cats, have a reflective layer at the back of the eye that helps to increase its efficiency after dark. When looking directly at a light, such as headlights, their eyes reflect the light and shine in the dark.

Grass snake

Adder

Eyes without eyelids
Snakes have no eyelids. A transparent disc of skin protects the eye and is regularly sloughed with the rest of the skin. Adders have vertical rectangular pupils, grass snakes and smooth snakes circular pupils, but the reason for the difference is not known.

Night

Day

Eyes that see by day or night
A cat's eyes, like those of all land animals, each have a central part, or pupil, that is always black and acts as a window, letting light pass into the eye. In the dark the pupil expands to let in as much light as possible. In the light it contracts to protect the sensitive region at the back of the eye from receiving too much light. A cat's pupils contract to vertical slits, but those of most animals are round when contracted.

Brown rat

Whiskers that show the way
Rats – like cats and many other animals that spend a lot of time moving about in the dark – have long, sensitive whiskers on the nose so they can feel their way where the light is too poor to see well. Cats also have whiskers on their brows – some on their elbows too. Moles have sensitive hairs on the tail that let them feel their way backwards along their tunnels without bumping into anything.

Eyes of a different colour
The fox is unusual in having an amber, or golden-orange, iris (the part of the eye surrounding the pupil). Most cats have a green iris, but in many animals it is dark brown, giving an impression of all-black eyes and making it difficult to tell if the pupil is expanded or contracted.

Eyes with rectangular pupils
Sheep and goats have pupils that are rectangular and horizontal. No one knows for certain whether the animals gain any advantage from this. Toads also have pupils of similar shape when contracted.

Eyes that are small and weak
Despite the expression 'blind as a bat', bats' eyes see well enough to aid them in navigation. Even the mole's two tiny eyes are not blind, as is often believed; they can tell dark from light, and can also recognise movement.

Long-eared bat

Grey squirrel

Red deer

Eyes for judging leaps
Squirrels need to judge distances accurately when leaping among tree branches, so their eyes face more to the front than those of most other rodents. They also have short noses that do not get in the way when they look directly forwards.

Eyes for stalking prey
Predators such as weasels need to focus on their prey, so their eyes face more to the front than animals with all-round vision. Each eye has a field of vision that considerably overlaps with that of the other eye; this gives three-dimensional vision and permits the accurate judgment of distances. But the head must be turned to scan an area.

Weasel

Eyes for seeing all round
Animals that live or feed in the open, such as deer, sheep and rabbits, need all-round vision so they can keep watch for danger even with their heads down while feeding. Their eyes are long-sighted and set at the side of the head so that they can scan about 300° – to the front, sides and most of the rear – without turning the head. But they see less detail than human eyes.

SCENT

MOST LAND ANIMALS have a much more sensitive and discriminating sense of smell than humans. Smell is the sense they use most – to find food and water, follow trails and recognise each other. Many animals, mammals especially, produce particular scents to aid communication; they are made in scent glands – often by the activity of bacteria – in various parts of the body, such as under the root of the tail. The scent secretions are often greasy so that they will last and not be washed away by the first rain.

Dogs secrete scent in their urine which reveals their sex and identity to other dogs that sniff it. The sniffer can also tell whether the scent is new or old. Many animals, carnivores especially, use scent to mark territory. Badgers, which live in 'clans', mark each other with scent to tell clan members from outsiders, and to recognise individual clan members. Some animals, such as weasels and grass snakes, use scent as a defence. When attacked, they eject a foul-smelling scent to distract the assailant.

Scent from the feet
Dogs scratch at the ground to mark territory with scent from glands between the toes. Some deer – fallow, for example – have scent glands in the cleft of each hind foot; their secretions probably convey messages to other deer.

Noctule bat

Scent from the face
Most bats have scent glands on the face, but on the noctule bat they are particularly noticeable. The secretions are strong-smelling and greasy, and may help sex and roost identification. Probably the female also recognises her own baby in the dark by its scent.

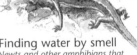

Common newt

Finding water by smell
Newts and other amphibians that hibernate on land make their way to ponds each spring to breed. They seem able to find their way to the water by its smell.

Dalmatian

Hunting by scent
Like all snakes, the grass snake constantly flicks out its tongue to 'taste' the air or ground in front of it and find its way about. In this way it detects the scent of prey.

Scent from the chin
A rabbit rubs the large scent gland under its chin against saplings, posts, stones or the ground, to mark them as part of its territory. Cats also use their chin or forehead to rub their scent against familiar objects.

Scent from the tail
Otters are among the many animals that leave scent marks as claims to territory. They often scent their droppings with secretions from glands under the tail, or sometimes rub their haunches on stones or logs to smear scent on them.

Messages between mates
When male red deer or sheep stretch out their necks and pull back their lips, they are sampling the air to detect scents. This behaviour, called 'flehmen', is common in hoofed mammals, which do it most at breeding time to tell when a potential mate is in season.

Red deer

Scenting the air
When a fox waves its bushy tail, it may be wafting out scent from the gland on its upper surface. A squirrel's tail may perform a similar role. Squirrels certainly twitch their tails frequently when agitated or displaying to a rival.

Singling out the baby
Most mothers will suckle only their own young. Ewes, cow seals and other animals that breed among large groups recognise their own baby in a crowd of others by its individual smell.

HEARING

MOST ANIMALS NEED acute hearing to survive. They must constantly listen to be aware of danger or to detect prey, especially at night when vision is limited. Often, mammals can move each ear independently, scanning all round while keeping still and undetected.

Many animals can hear ultrasonic sounds – sounds too high-pitched for human ears. Bats have the best-developed hearing of all, and for them it largely takes the place of vision. A bat with its ears experimentally plugged with cotton wool is almost helpless and will fly only with extreme reluctance. Yet blindfolded bats can fly and catch food with little difficulty. Snakes are deaf, having neither ears nor eardrums. They are sensitive to vibrations through the ground.

In the wild, mammals are silent most of the time because it is safer not to attract unwelcome attention. Most, though, will growl, squeak, hiss or scream if attacked or frightened. Some species have special calls to communicate with others of their kind – calling a mate, for example.

The talking foxes
Foxes commonly bark, yap or howl at night to communicate with each other. They have a dozen or more distinctive calls, each with its own meaning, and are especially noisy in winter, during the breeding season.

Listening for prey
Predators such as the pine marten tend to have forward facing ears that can focus on the same area as their forward facing eyes, so bringing two senses at once to inspect in detail the scene ahead.

Squeaks as tracking signals
Nestling mice and other rodents give out tiny squeaks too high-pitched for humans to hear. The squeaks help the mother to find young that stray from the nest and keep the family together in the days before their eyes open.

Common dormouse

Listening for danger
The black rat's ears are constantly twitching to detect the slightest sound, especially when it is feeding. It needs to be alert to danger, such as a prowling cat. Like mice, rabbits and other animals preyed on by carnivores, it has large ears.

Calling a mate
Like other male frogs, male marsh frogs croak loudly at breeding time to attract females. Large vocal sacs amplify the voice to carry over a wide area. Frogs have no ear flap, but there is a large, sensitive eardrum behind the eye.

Snarling a warning
Dogs, like many other mammals, snarl and grind their teeth to warn off other animals. Often they also use visual signals such as erect fur, bared teeth and a crouching posture ready for springing to the attack.

Long-eared bat

Horseshoe bats

Hunting by echoes
Bats emit ultrasonic sounds and locate prey (or obstacles in their path) when the sounds bounce back. Horseshoe bats emit sound through the nostrils that is directed and focused by the fleshy flap round the nose. Ordinary bats such as the long-eared emit sound through clenched teeth. All bats have relatively large ears in order to catch the slightest echo.

Bellowing for mastery
Red deer stags bellow loudly at rutting time to intimidate rivals and win the notice of females. The stags that bellow longest and most often acquire the largest harems. Fallow bucks and sika stags behave in a similar way.

BREEDING

IN WILD ANIMALS, breeding is linked to the seasons. This ensures that the young are produced at the most advantageous time of year, when food is plentiful. In some mammals (badgers, stoats, grey seals, roe deer), the egg does not begin to develop in the womb as soon as it is fertilised but starts after a delay of some weeks. This allows courting and mating to take place at a convenient time but ensures that the young are born when conditions are best.

Grey seals, for example, gather on shore in large herds for breeding each autumn, and mating takes place soon after the birth of pups from last year's mating. The young seals take only about 250 days to develop, so if the egg were implanted at once, pups would be born well before the next autumn gathering. But implantation is delayed roughly 100 days so that the pups are born at the most advantageous time.

Young born in the open
For larger mammals, such as fallow deer, making a nest and rearing a large family is not feasible. The young are born in the open, usually only one each year, and have a full covering of fur or hair. They open their eyes at birth and are quickly able to walk and run.

Bank vole

Young born in a nest or den
Voles and other small mammals give birth to blind, naked young. The mother selects a sheltered place to build a nest in which the large litter is kept warm and protected for a number of weeks until the young are developed sufficiently to survive outdoors.

Care from the father

A male fox will bring food to the den to help to feed the female and her cubs. This is unusual; the males of most mammals play no part in rearing the young.

Young hatched from eggs

Frogs, toads and newts lay eggs covered in jelly (spawn) in water. Reptiles lay eggs enclosed in a shell or membrane. Some, the grass snake, for example, leave them in a warm place. In others, such as the adder, the eggs hatch inside the female so that live, active young are born.

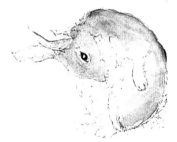

Preparing a breeding nest

Breeding nests are made by the female, generally from plant material. A doe rabbit plucks fur from her own chest to make a warm lining for the nest chamber of her burrow. The fur comes out easily because of hormone changes during pregnancy.

Young reared on milk

The grey seal, like all mammals, suckles its young on milk, which provides nourishment in the form of fats, sugars and proteins, and also helps to combat infection. All mammals care for their young until they are old enough to fend for themselves.

SLEEPING AND FEEDING

ALL ANIMALS NEED to rest and sleep, and to do so in a safe place, such as within a herd or hidden in a nest or burrow. Safety, temperature and the availability of food all play a part in deciding when an animal is active and when it rests.

Most land animals sleep or rest by day and seek food in the dark. Larger animals such as deer have less need to worry about predators so can sleep at any time. Although some animals, such as shrews, need to eat almost constantly to live, others do not necessarily eat every day. Snakes, for example, can live for a week or so on one meal. With cold-blooded animals – snakes, lizards and amphibians – activity depends on body temperature. Lizards and snakes rely on the heat of the sun so are out only in daylight, and inactive in cold weather. Frogs and toads can move about more in the cold than reptiles, and can be active at night.

Many animals feed well in autumn to build up fat reserves for winter, when food is scarce. Some, such as dormice, then spend winter in hibernation – hidden in a safe place with their body functions slowed down.

Wood mouse

Safety in daylight
Squirrels are among the few wild mammals active only by day. Their food is easy to find in daylight, and leaping from branch to branch is safer when they can see where they are going. In the tree tops they have little to fear from predators, so have less need to be nocturnal than mice, for example.

Safety in darkness
Wood mice, like other small mammals, are vulnerable to predators, and venture out only in the dark. Voles live among dense cover so can risk going out by day as well as by night.

Red squirrels

Food by night
Hedgehogs, although they have little to fear from predators, come out mostly at night. This is because they feed mainly on nocturnal creatures such as worms, slugs and beetles.

Common seals

Life with the tide
Seals are active by day and night and sleep at any time, on land or in the water. The state of the tide, not light and darkness, rules their lives. They feed more often at high tide, searching the shallows for crabs and flatfish. When the tide is low, they often find convenient spots to come ashore and rest.

Day and night activity
Shrews use up so much energy that they have to replenish it by eating frequently. They are active both day and night, and alternately rest and forage every few hours. To avoid predators they normally stay out of sight in burrows or under dense vegetation.

Common shrew

Sleeping through winter
Bats, like hedgehogs and dormice, hibernate in winter because their food supply is scarce in cold weather. By staying inactive with a low body temperature they conserve energy and reduce their need for food. Bats hibernate most efficiently in places with an even temperature of 2-6°C. If the site they first choose gets too warm or too cold as winter progresses, they may wake up and move to a more suitable place. Horseshoe bats, especially, need places that are also damp.

Horseshoe bats

A regular routine below ground
To the mole in its dark tunnels there can be little difference between night and day. It has several spells of activity within a 24 hour period – perhaps three or four, with rests between. But activity often occurs at similar times in successive 24 hour periods, suggesting that moles are not totally insensitive to time rhythms.

IDENTIFYING ANIMALS

ALL THE ANIMALS described in this book live on land or at the water's edge. Many are shy, nocturnal or rare – often all three – so may be glimpsed only briefly. To aid recognition, this identification key shows animals as they might appear at first glance, and they have been grouped according to their individual characteristics. The key gives an indication of size and appearance and, in some cases, where the animal might be seen, as well as where to find it in the book.

Size is crucial in identification – note how an animal compares in size with a familiar creature such as a cat. Where it is and what it is doing are also useful clues to identity. Many smaller animals are most often seen only when dead. This gives a good opportunity to study their colour, fur texture and other features missed in a brief glimpse.

CARNIVORES PAGES 34-73

All are flesh eaters, including fish-eating seals.
Many also eat other foods such as fruit and insects.

FOX *Pages 34-39*
Looks like a slim, pointed-eared dog, but with a very bushy tail. Often seen by day in all sorts of country and in suburban areas.

CATS *Pages 40-43*
Striped, bushy-tailed, tabby-like wild cats are found only in Scotland. Feral cats (domestic cats living wild) occur all over Britain.

Wild cat

BADGER *Pages 62-67*
Resembles a stockily built dog, with short legs and striped face. Active mainly at night in woods, meadows, moorland.

PINE MARTEN *Pages 54-55*
Looks like a short-legged cat with a thick tail. An uncommon forest and moorland animal. Rarely seen by day.

OTTER *Pages 56-61*
A long, slim, flat-headed animal that swims and dives well. Found in undisturbed places in or near water. Scarce, except in Scotland and Ireland.

POLECAT *Pages 52-53*
The size of a small, short-legged cat. Found in Wales. Paler forms elsewhere are probably polecat-ferrets.

MINK *Pages 50-51*
A bushy-tailed waterside animal that swims and dives well. Often seen by day. Smaller than an otter.

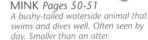

STOAT *Pages 46-47*
Rat-sized, with a long body that undulates as it bounds. Often seen on moors, farmland, roads and verges.

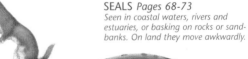

SEALS *Pages 68-73*
Seen in coastal waters, rivers and estuaries, or basking on rocks or sand-banks. On land they move awkwardly.

WEASEL *Pages 48-49*
Looks like an elongated mouse. Often seen streaking across a road. Also moves in undulating bounds.

Grey seal

HOOFED MAMMALS PAGES 74-111
Long-legged animals that feed on grass and leaves.
All except ponies have cloven hoofs.

Red deer

Muntjac

Exmoor pony

HALF-WILD PONIES Pages 74-77
Unshod breeding herds inhabit moors and forests, especially in south and west of England and Wales. All have owners. Colours are very variable.

DEER Pages 78-105
Long-legged animals that range from muntjac (springer-spaniel size) to pony-sized red deer. Most males have antlers, but not all year. Seen wild or in parks.

FERAL GOAT Pages 106-7
Looks like a shaggy sheep with widely spread horns. Found on cliffs or mountainsides, in north and west.

WILD BOAR Pages 110-11
Dark and bristly, and much leaner than domestic pigs. Males are bigger than females, with sharp tusks in both jaws.

SOAY SHEEP Pages 108-9
Brown with coiled horns. Found wild on some Hebridean islands. Some half-wild herds in England.

MARSUPIALS PAGES 112-13
Kangaroo-like animals that carry their young in a pouch. None native to Britain but a few imported animals have escaped to live in the wild.

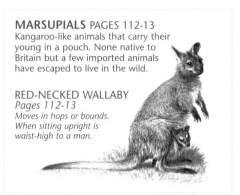

RED-NECKED WALLABY
Pages 112-13
Moves in hops or bounds. When sitting upright is waist-high to a man.

HARES AND RABBITS PAGES 150-61
Long-eared animals with short tails. Their long hind feet give them a hopping or bounding gait. They are normally active by day or night.

HARES
Pages 150-3
Look like large rabbits with big, staring eyes. Live above ground.

Brown hare

RABBIT *Pages 156-61*
Usually found in colonies, mostly in lowlands. Often seen near the burrow in which it lives.

INSECTIVORES PAGES 162-81
Animals of varied appearance but very similar internal structure. All eat insects, but also worms, slugs and other small creatures.

MOLE
Pages 162-5
Hamster size. Has large, heavily clawed forefeet.

HEDGEHOG *Pages 168-71*
The size of a guinea pig. Has a spiny coat. Seen in farms and gardens, sometimes by day.

Common shrew

SHREWS *Pages 174-81*
Smaller than mice, and with long noses. Highly active; squeak loudly.

RODENTS PAGES 114-49

Gnawing animals, mainly active at night. Alike in having large front teeth that grow constantly.

Brown rat

MICE Pages 120-9
Small, with long, thin tails, and big eyes and ears. Found indoors and outdoors.

Wood mouse

Field vole

RATS Pages 116-19
Have thick, scaly tails, and big eyes and ears. Usually in or near buildings. Brown rat common in hedgerows.

VOLES Pages 130-4
Slightly bigger than mice. Chubby and round-faced with short tails, and ears buried in fur.

Common dormouse

Grey squirrel

ALIEN RODENTS Pages 148-9
Many pet hamsters and gerbils, and other foreign species from zoos, escape and establish wild colonies.

DORMICE Pages 136-9
Have fluffy tails and big eyes. Come out only at night, climbing among trees and bushes.

SQUIRRELS Pages 140-7
Bushy-tailed and rat-sized. Seen by day in or near trees. Grey species widespread, red mainly in north and west.

Hamster

BATS PAGES 182-205
Flying mammals with mouse-sized, furry bodies. At rest they hang head down in trees, lofts and caves.

HORSESHOE BATS
Pages 182-7
Have horseshoe-shaped skin round nostrils. Out only at night.

Lesser horseshoe bat

ORDINARY BATS
Pages 188-203
Have dog-like muzzles and dark or pinkish faces. Out only at night.

Natterer's bat

AMPHIBIANS AND REPTILES PAGES 206–31
Amphibians live in damp places and lay their eggs in water. Reptiles are able to live in drier places and bear their young, or lay eggs, on land.

FROGS *Pages 206-9*
Amphibians with smooth, moist skin and long hind legs with feet fully webbed. Move in leaps.

TOADS *Pages 210-13*
Amphibians with rough, warty skin, drier than a frog's. Hind feet only partly webbed. Normally crawl.

NEWTS *Pages 214-15*
Lizard-like amphibians with smooth skin. Tail flattened at sides. Walk slowly with wriggling movement.

SNAKES *Pages 218-23*
Limbless reptiles with dry, scaly skin and no eyelids. Move with a gliding motion from side to side.

LIZARDS *Pages 224-7*
Small reptiles with dry, scaly skin. Tail rounded. Move with swift, darting wriggle.

SLOW-WORM *Pages 228-9*
A snake-like legless lizard with smooth, dry, shiny skin. Unlike snake, has eyelids. Often found in compost heaps.

ANIMALS

FOX

FOXES ARE RESOURCEFUL and thrive in many places. Mostly at night, but also by day, they scavenge from carcasses or kill small mammals, especially rabbits and field voles. In summer they catch many beetles, and in autumn feed on fruit. Foxes in coastal areas forage for crabs and dead fish or sea birds.

Alert and wary, foxes have acute hearing and a keen sense of smell, and eyes that are quick to spot movement. From October to January a fox has a full, thick coat, while for most of the summer it moults. Although foxes are mostly seen alone, they live in family groups usually made up of a dog fox (male), a breeding vixen (female) and her cubs, and perhaps one or two non-breeding vixens from old litters. An earth or den, perhaps in a rock crevice or under tree roots, is used at breeding time. The vixen may dig an earth or enlarge an abandoned burrow. At other times, foxes shelter above ground. Few live more than eight years.

Although foxes from the same group forage alone, they may meet during the night for play or mutual grooming.

About May foxes begin to moult their winter coats, and scratch to remove loose fur. The moult spreads slowly along the back and hindquarters.

Fox

Vulpes vulpes

65cm body; 38cm tail

Widespread and abundant in many habitats, from city streets to mountains.

The rump is often silvery with white-tipped hairs.

Amber eyes

Coat may vary from yellow-brown to red-brown.

Bushy tail with white tip

Lower legs and the backs of the ears are black

Prey such as voles may be detected by sound. The fox leaps on the spot the sound came from, pinning the prey with its forepaws.

Surplus food is often buried for later. The fox uses its forefeet to dig a hole, and its nose to push soil over the cache.

Rearing fox cubs

FOXES BREED ONCE a year. The mating season lasts from Christmas until about February, when courting foxes may be heard emitting short triple barks, or shattering the silence of the night with unearthly screams as a vixen calls to a potential mate. The dog and vixen hunt and travel together for about three weeks, towards the end of which they may mate several times. The vixen is pregnant for about 53 days, with the peak period for births around mid March.

A litter of cubs is born on the bare soil of the den or earth; the vixen makes no nest. The cubs open their eyes at 10-14 days, and take their first solid food – often regurgitated by their mother – at three to four weeks. A week later they emerge from the den, and their dark brown cub coats start to change colour. By about eight weeks the

During the mating season the dog fox, tail held straight out, will follow the vixen for long periods. They may be seen during the daytime.

Four-week-old cub

Eight-week-old cub

Cubs grow rapidly. At four or five weeks old their blue eyes slowly change to amber and their coats begin to go reddish-brown.

coat is red-brown. Non-breeding vixens may help to rear the cubs. The cubs stay together as a family throughout summer, reaching adult size about September. Young vixens may stay with the family group, but young dog foxes leave in autumn or winter to find their own territories.

The vixen stays in the den or earth with her cubs until they are two weeks old, the dog fox bringing her food. After that she spends more time outside.

A litter of four or five round-faced, short-eared cubs is born in March or April. They are born blind and are covered with fur of a deep chocolate brown.

As the cubs grow up, they fight and squabble. Sparring cubs stand on their hind legs and push each other.

At the end of the year, some of the cubs leave to find their own territories. An adult will sometimes drive a young fox away from the group.

If disturbed, the vixen moves the cubs to another earth. Cubs up to six weeks old are carried in her mouth, one at a time, each held by the scruff of the neck.

Foxes in town

THERE ARE FOXES in most towns and cities
from the south up to Nottingham. They are
commonest in suburbs, especially those built in
the 1930s. In northern England and Wales urban
foxes are much scarcer. There are some in Scotland
– in Edinburgh and Glasgow – and also in Ireland –
in Belfast and some cities of the Republic.

Town foxes usually rest by day, perhaps under a
garden shed or in a sunny spot on a roof. At night they
forage over a small area, mostly for scraps, windfalls or
worms, but occasionally taking a pet rabbit or guinea pig.
A vixen chooses her breeding den in late winter, often
under a shed or a pile of rubbish, or she may dig an earth.
Cubs may play outside from late April or early May, and
some will readily take food from the hand. From late June
the cubs nest above ground during hot weather, behind a
bush or similar spot, and the den is gradually abandoned.

1 *A fox may rob
a bird table of crusts
or bacon rind if it is
easy to climb or leap
on. Worms often
surface on a lawn on
a warm, damp night,
providing a feast for
a foraging fox.*

2 The cavity under a garden shed provides a den for a litter of fox cubs. Foxes and cats rarely bother each other. If there is a confrontation, the fox is quite likely to back down first.

4 Foxes are scavengers and do raid dustbins – but not as often as is generally believed.

3 A suburban back garden after dark may be a hunting ground for one or two foxes, or their permanent home. They prefer a garden that is not too tidy, with plenty of shrubs or clutter for shelter.

WILD CAT

REMOTE HIGHLAND FORESTS and moors are the home of the wild cat. It was persecuted as vermin and almost died out in the 19th century, surviving only in isolated areas north of Scotland's Great Glen. Since the 1920s it has been slowly spreading south again.

Wild cats are most active at dawn and dusk, hunting alone or in pairs. Rabbits, mountain hares, small rodents and birds are their main food. The cats either lie in ambush to pounce on their prey, or stalk it and then attack with a rush. They usually keep to one mate, but spend much of their time alone and normally breed only once a year. Second litters born in late summer are probably the offspring of wild and feral cat hybrids. Young wild cats are independent at about five months and fully grown by about ten months. They live for up to 12 years.

The female is pregnant for 65 days. There are usually four kittens in a litter, born in May, who emerge from the den after about four or five weeks. They start learning to hunt with their mother when about nine weeks old and are weaned at about four months.

When a wild cat scratches a tree it may not be just to sharpen its claws or stretch. It may also be marking its territory with scent secreted by its foot glands.

Wild cat

Felis silvestris

70cm body; 30cm tail

Found in Highlands. Spread south masked by interbreeding with feral cats.

Blunt, rounded tail-tip with three to five dark rings

Although it resembles a domestic tabby, the wild cat is slightly larger with longer, softer fur.

Black or grey body stripes

The den is sited where there is a good view of the area around. It may be in a rock pile, an old fox earth or under a tree stump.

Before mating, the male will follow the female and nuzzle her flanks. In Britain wild cats mate in the first two weeks in March.

FERAL CAT

FERAL CATS ARE domestic cats that have reverted to living wild. Some are lost or abandoned pets; others are descendants of such pets and have always lived wild. They usually live in colonies of related animals. In rural areas there are small colonies in farm outbuildings, but most live in towns – not in residential areas where pet cats are numerous, but in the grounds of places such as hospitals, as well as in factories, dockyards and even city squares. An average colony has about 15 cats, but some are much larger.

A feral cat colony establishes an order of rank among its members and claims its own territory, driving out other cats. Females outnumber males by about three to two, and each year a female may bear three or four litters of about three kittens. Many kittens die of cat flu and other diseases, or in accidents. Rural cats feed mainly on small mammals and birds. Cats in built-up areas feed mostly by scavenging for household and restaurant waste.

Many farmyard cats are feral, hunting for their own food.

Members of a cat colony rub against one another to transfer scent from a gland on the top of the head. This helps them to recognise one another.

Feral cat

Felis (domestic)

50cm body; 30cm tail

May be present in any part of Britain. Usually most numerous in urban areas.

Pointed
tail

Most wild-born animals
are pure black, black with white
markings or tabby. Feral tabbies
are more blotched than true wild
cats and have pointed tails.
Size varies greatly.

Tabby blotching

Prominent places
in the territory
are scent-marked
by rubbing with
a gland under
the chin, or by
spraying urine.

Urban feral
cats will hunt
small birds and
mammals to
add to their
diet of scraps.

Creamy-yellow throat

Black legs

Dark mask

Polecat-ferret
No distinct mask

Polecat
Mustela putorius
Head and body 36cm
Coat paler in winter
Page 52

Legs may be dark or pale.

Bushy tail

Pine marten
Martes martes
Head and body 45cm
Page 54

Ferret
Page 52

No mask

Pale legs

Pink eyes

Identifying stoats, weasels and relatives

THE WEASEL, stoat, pine marten, polecat, mink and otter are all members of the weasel family, and resemble each other in build, colouring or behaviour. All are active hunters with long, sinuous bodies and fairly short legs. They often sit upright to look round, and can move fast, bounding along with an arched back. Males are up to 50 per cent bigger than females.

Confusion is most likely between the squirrel-sized stoat and the smaller weasel. It is possible to confuse the pine marten, polecat and mink, and perhaps also a swimming mink and swimming otter – the otter is much larger, but its size is not obvious in the water. But each has distinguishing characteristics, and usually can also be identified from its habitat, though the stoat and weasel are found in most types of country. The mink and otter are likely to be seen in or near water, the polecat on farmland or lower hill slopes and the pine marten only in remote northern forests or moors. Except for the stoat and weasel all are fairly uncommon – the pine marten and otter are rare – and are active mainly at night.

Pastel mink
Page 50

May be pale grey,
buff or white.

Stoat
Mustela erminea
Head and body 25cm
Page 46

Stoat in
ermine

Looks black at
a distance.

Mink
Mustela vison
Head and body 40cm
Page 50

Glossy coat

Black tip to tail

Crisp line
between
brown
and white

A swimming mink
has a narrow head
and swims jerkily.

A swimming otter has
a broad head and swims
smoothly.

Brown
throat-patches

Irregular line between
brown and white

Weasel
Mustela nivalis
Head and body 20cm
Page 48

Short tail
with plain tip

Broad flat
head

Heavy, tapered
tail

Otter
Lutra lutra
*Head and
body 90cm*
Page 56

Webbed feet

STOAT

SLIM AND SAVAGE, the stoat is one of the fiercest of predators, active by day or night. It relentlessly tracks down its prey by scent.

The stoat has suffered at the hands of gamekeepers but remains numerous and widely distributed. Its biggest threat to survival was the introduction of the myxomatosis disease in the 1950s, which wiped out almost all rabbits in Britain. But as the stoat eats many things beside rabbits it survived in most parts. A stoat's hunting ground usually covers about 20ha (50 acres). Its den is in a rock crevice or abandoned rabbit burrow, and it normally lives alone. Stoats mate in summer, but implantation of the fertilised egg is delayed until the following March, females giving birth in April or May. Young stoats, independent at about 12 weeks old, may be mistaken for weasels but can be recognised by the black tail-tip.

In Ireland, stoats are darker and have a wavy dividing line between flank and belly fur.

There is one litter of six or more young a year. The young first leave the den at about five weeks old, and often hunt and play in a family group.

In north Scotland stoats turn creamy-white in winter, and are then called ermine. Elsewhere, stoats may go partially white and patchy. In south England and in Ireland, stoats often stay brown. The tail-tip always remains black.

Stoat

Mustela erminea

25cm body; 10cm tail

Widespread in woods, farms, uplands, despite extensive trapping and shooting.

Male

Female

The stoat, alert and inquisitive, often sits upright to view its surroundings.

The sexes look alike, but a full-grown male is up to 50 per cent bigger than a female.

Black
tail-tip

Creamy-white underparts

The stoat can move fast, perhaps up to 32km an hour in bounds of 50cm. It is seen usually where there is good cover. In farmland it keeps mainly to hedges, walls or fences.

WEASEL

THE WEASEL LOOKS a little like a long, slim, fast-moving mouse, and often moves in undulating bounds. It is the smallest British carnivore, and a fierce hunter by day or night. Mice are one of its main foods – one weasel may eat hundreds in a year. Territory size depends on the food available; where it is plentiful there is no need to hunt so far afield. A weasel eats about 33-36 per cent of its own weight in food a day.

Young weasels are born in April or May, and there may be a second litter in July or August. Youngsters stay with the mother, often hunting in family parties, until up to ten weeks old, when they are fully grown. Unlike other British carnivores, which do not breed in their first year, young weasels may breed during their first summer.

Few weasels live more than a year. Gamekeepers trap large numbers as vermin, and many are killed on the roads. Cats, owls, foxes and birds of prey will also kill weasels, but risk a hard fight in doing so.

Young weasels are born in a nest of leaves or grass in a hole or crevice. A litter usually numbers five or six. Their eyes open when they are about three weeks old.

Prey is usually taken on the ground, but weasels climb well and can raid a bird's nest box. Their slim bodies can squeeze through an opening only 3mm across.

Weasel

Mustela nivalis

20cm; 5cm tail

Widespread in most habitats, but absent from Ireland and many of the smaller islands.

Brown tail

The weasel's brown fur meets its white underparts in an irregular line along its flanks. Its coat does not go white in winter like the stoat's.

Brown throat-patch

Wavy flank line

Voles and mice are the main food, along with some rats and rabbits as well as small birds and their chicks if the chance arises. Prey is killed by a bite at the back of the neck.

Although a weasel hunts mainly by scent, it will attempt to seize a small bird such as a meadow pipit if it disturbs one into flight.

MINK

WHEN THE MINK was introduced to Britain from North America in the late 1920s, it was intended to be kept captive on fur farms and raised for its valuable pelt. But many mink escaped and bred in the wild. Since 1930 they have spread over most of Britain.

At first mink were assumed to be a pest and thousands were trapped, but with little noticeable effect. The mink now seems to be a permanent addition to Britain's wildlife, with few threats to its existence, but its acceptability is still a controversial issue. Mink eat a lot of fish, and their attacks on trout on a fish farm or valuable young salmon can have serious effects. They also eat water voles – one factor in the decline of this species. Although mink probably do not seriously compete with otters for food, they may prevent otters from recolonising suitable habitats.

Young mink are born in a den among waterside stones or tree roots. From June onwards they can be seen foraging with their mother, and are fully grown by autumn.

One litter of five or six young mink is produced a year. They leave the den at about two months old.

Mink swim well. Some of their food is caught in the water. Usually they take slower-moving prey such as eels and crayfish.

Mink

Mustela vison

40cm body; 12.5cm tail

A waterside animal becoming steadily more numerous and still extending its range.

Chocolate-brown fur

Rarely seen far from a river or lake, the mink is mostly active at night, often preying on waterfowl. Its dense, glossy, chocolate-brown fur looks almost black from a distance, especially when wet. Female usually smaller than male.

All wild mink are descended from animals that escaped from fur farms. Descendants of those bred to provide pale-coloured pelts may still be seen, and are known as pastel mink.

A swimming mink can be distinguished from a swimming otter by its more pointed snout, darker colouring and smaller size. It has a longer body and thicker tail than a water vole.

POLECAT

ONCE KNOWN AS the foul-mart because of its strong smell, the polecat used to be widespread but was ruthlessly trapped and killed for its fur (known as fitch) and because it was considered a threat to game and livestock. Trapping has declined and numbers are on the increase, but the picture is confused by the many ferrets living wild.

Ferrets are creamy-white, domesticated polecats used to catch rabbits, and some escape or are lost. Over time, many have reverted to polecat colouring and are known as polecat-ferrets; there are colonies in many areas, and they have also interbred with true polecats.

Polecats vary in colour as their long outer (guard) hairs range from creamy-yellow to near black, depending on how much ferret and how much true polecat is in their ancestry. Polecats are commonest on farmland and are mostly active at night. They often inhabit abandoned rabbit burrows. Some live to be five or more.

The male polecat is slightly larger than the female. They mate between March and May; courtship is rough, the male dragging the female by the scruff of the neck. Usually there is one litter a year.

Litters contain from five to ten young, born with white silky hair. Darker fur grows later, and the young leave the nest at two months, about August. Family groups may be seen together in late summer, but polecats are normally solitary.

The pea-sized stink glands on the underside, at the base of the tail, secrete a persistent, foul-smelling scent, used defensively or to mark a territorial boundary.

Polecat

Mustela putorius

38cm body; 14cm tail

Found mainly in Wales but spreading. Polecat-ferrets found throughout Britain.

Summer

In summer the woolly underfur is largely hidden by the guard hairs. In winter the denser underfur makes the guard hairs stick out, so the animal looks paler and rounder.

Winter

Polecat

Polecat-ferret

Ferret

A polecat has white ear tips and a dark mask. A polecat-ferret usually has a paler forehead and no mask. A pure ferret is creamy-white.

Dark mask

Dark guard hairs protect creamy-yellow woolly underfur.

PINE MARTEN

ONCE THE LITHE pine marten was widespread in Britain. Now it is uncommon, found mainly in remote forests or sometimes on rocky moorland where it spends much of its time on the ground looking for food in forest rides and grassy areas.

Pine martens breed only once a year, mating in July or August, though females do not become pregnant until about January after a delay in the implantation of the fertilised egg. A litter averages three babies, born in March or April in a den usually in a crevice among rocks or tree roots. The young spend at least five weeks in the den before their eyes open and they are big enough to venture out, and the family stays together until they are six months old. Youngsters grow quickly, reaching adult size in their first summer, but until their first winter moult they have paler, woollier fur than adults. Apart from man, the pine marten has no real enemy and can live up to ten years.

The pine marten is one of the few predators agile enough to catch a squirrel. If it falls, its lithe body twists to land safely on all fours from as high as 20m.

The marten climbs trees with ease. It grasps the trunk firmly, digs in its claws, and uses both hind legs together to force itself upwards in a series of jerky movements.

Pine marten

Martes martes

45cm; 23cm tail

Found in remote areas but is spreading into new forest plantations.

Male

Female

Creamy-yellow throat

Active mainly at night, the pine marten is rarely seen in daylight. It may be glimpsed as it crosses an open space such as a forest ride, and recognised by its distinctive bounding gait and bushy tail.

The pine marten, alert and elusive, is cat-size, with long rich brown fur and a bushy tail. Female slightly smaller than male.

Food is mostly from the ground – mainly small birds and mammals sought out by sight and smell. The marten also eats beetles, caterpillars, carrion, eggs and lots of berries.

OTTER

FEW EVER SEE a wild otter today, except perhaps on Scotland's west coast. Until the 1950s they could be found throughout most of Britain. Since then they have become rarer.

Otters live by undisturbed waters where there is plenty of cover, mostly by freshwater lakes, rivers or small streams, as well as some coasts. Fish are their main food. As much at home in the water as on land, otters are strong underwater swimmers, helped by large lungs and the ability to reduce their heart rate when diving and slow down oxygen consumption. They can focus their eyes to see easily underwater and have a moustache of stiff whiskers to help them to feel their way at the bottom of a muddy stream or in the dark; it may also help in detecting prey.

No one knows for sure how long they live in the wild, but captive otters have lived to be 20. Humans have been the otter's chief enemies, through hunting for sport and killing for fur or for fish protection. Otters are now fully protected and are slowly increasing in both numbers and distribution.

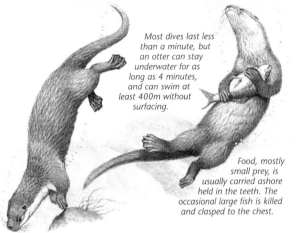

Most dives last less than a minute, but an otter can stay underwater for as long as 4 minutes, and can swim at least 400m without surfacing.

Food, mostly small prey, is usually carried ashore held in the teeth. The occasional large fish is killed and clasped to the chest.

Ears, eyes and nostrils set well to the top of the otter's head aid surface swimming. Its broad, flat head helps to distinguish it from a mink.

Otter

Lutra lutra

70cm body; 40cm tail

Scarce, except in Scotland. Populations slowly expanding in north and west. Now in scattered places in south and east.

A swimming otter makes a wide, V-shaped wake, only its head showing. It swims smoothly, its forelegs tucked up, but it paddles with them to manoeuvre or gain speed.

Small ears

Male

Female

The male, or dog, otter has a heavier head and thicker neck than the female (bitch) otter. She is also slightly smaller.

The otter is streamlined for speed in the water. It often stands upright to look around, balancing on its hind feet and tail.

Thick, tapered tail

Webbed feet

An otter eats with prey held in its forepaws. Fish are the main food, with eels a favourite. It also eats frogs, mammals and waterside birds.

A litter of cubs is born in a holt lined with grass or moss. Cubs have fine grey fur at birth. Their eyes open when they are from four to five weeks old.

Once their fluffy coats have changed to waterproof ones, the bitch teaches the cubs to swim. They often have to be encouraged – even pushed in.

Coastal otter families

THE REMOTENESS and abundant food of Scotland's west coast and islands make it the most popular part of Britain for otters. Whether found by coastal or inland waters, dog and bitch otters live separately, coming together only for mating, at any time of year. Courting otters usually find each other by scent – or by whistling to get each other's bearings. Before mating they often chase each other and pretend to fight, on land or in the water. The bitch is pregnant for about 62 days. The breeding den, or holt, is usually built in a quiet part of the bitch's territory. The cubs – usually two or three – are born blind and toothless, and weaned from about 12 weeks. They only develop an adult coat from two or three months.

The family breaks up when the cubs are about a year old, and the female begins to go on heat again. The cubs probably stay on the mother's territory for another few months before leaving, but may take several months to find permanent territories.

Frequent grooming keeps an otter's coat sleek and waterproof. Its thick underfur traps an insulating layer of air against its skin, and is kept dry underwater by the long outer fur.

Families often play together, on land or in the water. Lone otters sometimes toss pebbles and catch them in their mouths.

On the remote and rocky west coast of Scotland, otters are often seen by day. They feed on crabs, molluscs and various sea fishes.

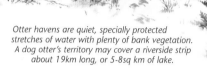

Otter havens are quiet, specially protected stretches of water with plenty of bank vegetation. A dog otter's territory may cover a riverside strip about 19km long, or 5-8sq km of lake.

Otter havens

EVEN WHERE FOOD is abundant, every otter needs a territory of several miles of undisturbed waterside with plenty of undergrowth. Since the 1950s riversides have been much altered by building and farming developments as well as by clearing for drainage. Water sports have also increasingly disturbed waterways.

All these have probably contributed to the otter's decline, but investigations during the 1960s suggested that the main reason was the increased use of pesticides, in particular aldrin and dieldrin. They cause water pollution and the contamination of fish with minute amounts of poison, which gradually accumulates in an otter eating a lot of them. A dog otter may eat 1-1.3kg of fish a day. Following withdrawal of the most dangerous pesticides, otters have begun to

1 *Scattered food remains such as fish scales mark the place where an otter has eaten a large fish.*

increase again, but in parts of central and southern England waters are still too polluted or disturbed to provide a safe home.

Otter havens may help to bring back the otter to lowland Britain. A number have been established by landowners in co-operation with conservationists, and where natural cover is sparse, artificial holts are sometimes built.

2 Otters catch the prey most readily available, generally coarse fish 10-20cm long. Large trout and salmon move too fast.

3 A steep snowy or muddy riverbank may be used as a slide by an otter family. The otters tuck up their forepaws and slide on their chests at speed into the water. They all repeat the game many times over.

4 The spraints (droppings) are used to mark territory, and left in conspicuous places such as on rocks and fallen trees.

5 Otter holts (dens) and lying-up places (sometimes called hovers) are usually under riverside tree roots.

BADGER

THERE ARE BADGERS in most parts of Britain, even in urban areas, notably on the south coast and in London, Bath and Bristol. Generally they are active at night and rarely seen. Badgers live in extensive burrow systems, or setts, dug out with their broad, powerful forepaws. Setts are usually in woodland, sometimes in fields or rubbish dumps, and include sleeping chambers with regularly changed bedding. Each sett is occupied by one or two families. The group forages within an established territory, defended against outsiders, which has well-defined paths between the sett, feeding grounds and latrines – dung pits dug singly or in groups.

Earthworms are the badger's main food, supplemented by cereals, beetles, fruit in autumn, and some mammals, particularly young rabbits dug out from their burrows. Badgers will also dig out and eat the contents of wasp and bee nests. A few badgers probably survive for up to 15 years.

Badgers keep to the same well-beaten paths through their territory. Wiry black-and-white hairs on a fence indicate a badger route. To prevent badgers tearing up rabbit-proof fencing, forestry fences may have special badger gates with heavy flaps.

Badgers use trees near the sett to sharpen their claws and clean mud off their paws, particularly on heavy soils. They prefer rough-barked trees such as elders and oaks.

In some areas, badgers will enter gardens to feed on household scraps, crops, windfall fruit or dustbin refuse, and may do damage.

Badger

Meles meles

76cm body; 15cm tail

Commonest in south and west. Scarce in East Anglia, parts of Scotland and urban Midlands.

Striped head

White-tipped ears

Straw, dry leaves, bracken or green plants are used as bedding. The badger gathers them between forepaws and chin and shuffles backwards to the sett entrance.

Strong forepaws

The badger emerges cautiously from its burrow (or sett), sniffing for danger, soon after dusk. Strong forepaws with long claws make it a powerful digger. The female is smaller than the male.

BADGERS, CATTLE AND TUBERCULOSIS

In parts of the south-west badger numbers are high, and setts are often close to cattle pastures. The incidence of tuberculosis is five times greater in the south-west than elsewhere, though less than one cow in a thousand is affected.

In spring territorial disputes are frequent, and badly bitten boars may contract tuberculosis through infected saliva.

IN 1971 A DEAD BADGER in Gloucestershire was found to be infected with the bacteria that cause tuberculosis in cattle. Since then, infected badgers have turned up in various parts of south-west England and occasionally elsewhere. The lungs and kidneys are particularly prone to infection, so a badger may spread the bacteria through its breath, urine and droppings. Tuberculosis can spread rapidly – in a few areas, up to 20 per cent of the badger population may have tuberculosis. Infected animals can survive for a long time and spread the disease widely.

Infected cattle suffer most from lung, not kidney, tuberculosis, probably catching it by sniffing at foraging badgers or at pasture contaminated by them. Despite stringent official efforts to eliminate tuberculosis in cows, it has persisted in the south-west. From 1975, badger setts in the region were gassed in an attempt to stamp out the disease, but the gassing campaign was stopped in 1982 because it was ineffective. Many farmers, though, believe that similar culls are necessary to control tuberculosis.

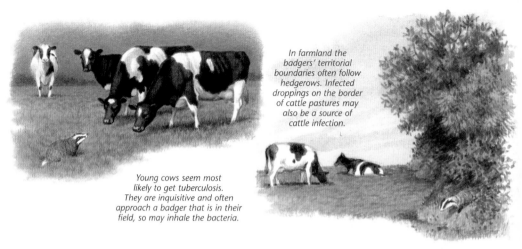

In farmland the badgers' territorial boundaries often follow hedgerows. Infected droppings on the border of cattle pastures may also be a source of cattle infection.

Young cows seem most likely to get tuberculosis. They are inquisitive and often approach a badger that is in their field, so may inhale the bacteria.

Infected badgers may lose condition and behave oddly. Attracted by cattle cake in troughs, some enter farm buildings. This may spread the disease.

Urine or saliva from an infected badger foraging for worms may contaminate pasture.

A badger community

A BADGER COMMUNITY usually includes a number of adult boars and sows and one or two litters of cubs, up to 15 animals. Setts are often dug in sloping ground or under a rocky overhang, generally in woods or copses. Large setts may have more than 40 entrances.

There is usually one main sett, with outlying setts around a territory of up to 40-50ha (100-125 acres). The main sett is a network of tunnels and chambers on several levels, usually within about 1m of the surface. Entrance holes are about 30cm wide.

2 *Badgers often play together and groom each other. Mutual grooming may involve two badgers or several.*

3 *Fallen trees near the sett provide both a playground and a food source. Badgers like to climb along them and to extract beetles, slugs and snails from under rotting bark.*

1 *Elder bushes and nettles often grow near setts. Badgers eat elderberries and disperse seeds in their droppings. Soil enriched with dung favours elder and nettle growth.*

6 Half-grown cubs enjoy long play periods around the sett, chasing and jumping on each other. Adults often join in.

8 A scratching tree has sets of parallel claw marks roughly 8mm apart.

7 The cubs – usually two or three in a litter – are born in a lined breeding chamber, where they remain for about eight weeks.

4 Outside each sett entrance there is a mound of excavated soil, compacted from years of use. Old bedding may also be left outside the hole.

5 Close to the main sett there is usually at least one latrine – a number of dung pits covering several square metres. Often the ground around has been scratched up by badgers.

Badgers mate between February and October, with the peak season in spring. The fertilised egg is then not implanted until December and cubs are born from mid January to mid March. They are blind until about five weeks old and weaning starts at 12 weeks. Some cubs stay with the family group, others leave, usually after their first winter, to find new territories.

In autumn, badgers lay down a large amount of fat under their skin, increasing in weight by up to 60 per cent. They then live mainly off this fat from mid December to mid February when activity is reduced.

COMMON SEAL

ALTHOUGH COMMON SEALS are often seen in groups of more than 100 basking contentedly in the sun, they are not really social animals. Unlike grey seals, they do not live in organised herds, and are placid rather than noisy, even at breeding time.

Common seals tend to be found on sandbanks around sheltered shores such as estuaries and sea lochs. They will sometimes haul themselves onto seaweed-covered rocks close to deep water to bask, often returning to the same place day after day. On sandbanks they allow the outgoing tide to strand them on the highest point, a good lookout position where they may stay for several hours. If disturbed they move close to the water's edge, ready for a quick getaway. They have good eyesight, on land or underwater. About a third of the British population live around The Wash but they travel long distances along the east coast, following fish shoals. They can live for 20-30 years.

The forelimb is a flipper with five long black claws, normally held close to the body. It acts as a stabiliser in the water.

When wet, the seal looks much slimmer and almost black. On land it moves with an awkward, humping motion, hardly using its fore flippers and not using its hind ones at all.

In the water the seal's rounded head looks like a buoy or fishing float. Its short muzzle and V-shaped nostrils help to distinguish it from a grey seal, which has almost parallel nostrils.

Common seal

Phoca vitulina

175cm long

May be seen off south coast but does not breed there. Rare off west of England, Wales.

Fish are the main food, caught mostly by diving to search the seabed. Flatfish and other bottom-dwelling fish are taken. Young seals may eat shrimps.

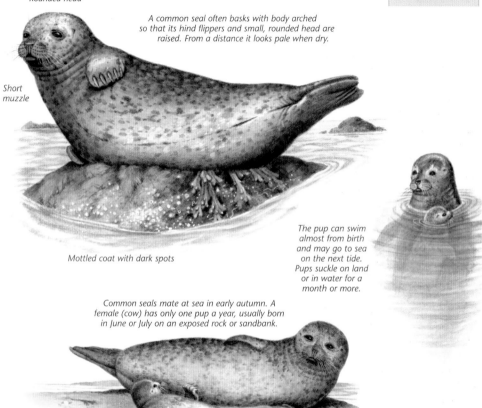

Rounded head

A common seal often basks with body arched so that its hind flippers and small, rounded head are raised. From a distance it looks pale when dry.

Short muzzle

Mottled coat with dark spots

The pup can swim almost from birth and may go to sea on the next tide. Pups suckle on land or in water for a month or more.

Common seals mate at sea in early autumn. A female (cow) has only one pup a year, usually born in June or July on an exposed rock or sandbank.

GREY SEAL

GREY (OR ATLANTIC) seals may be seen off most of Britain's coasts but are most numerous around Scotland, particularly the offshore islands. They gather to breed on shore, sometimes in their hundreds, from September to December. Outside the breeding season the seals spend much of their time at sea, sometimes for weeks on end, but haul themselves onto rocks or the shore for an occasional bask. While moulting, about March, the seals rest for long periods on rocks above high-tide level. Newly moulted seals are easily spotted because of their bright coats.

Fish are the seals' main food, adults eating a daily average of about 6kg, although they do not feed every day. Seal colonies on places like the Farne Islands have become overcrowded, causing damage to the soil and disease among pups. Because of their large numbers and fish consumption, and because they carry parasites transmitted to fish, there have been attempts at regular licensed culling (selective killing). These aroused so much public hostility that grey seals are now mostly left alone.

Cow seals are paler than bulls, especially when their fur is dry, and not nearly as heavy – only about half a bull's weight. They are also shorter in the muzzle and thinner in the neck.

The top of the seal's head is flat. Grey seals are often noisy, barking, hooting, moaning, hissing and snarling, on land and in water.

Grey seal

Halichoerus grypus

180-210cm long

Commonest around rocky shores, mainly off north and west coasts of Britain

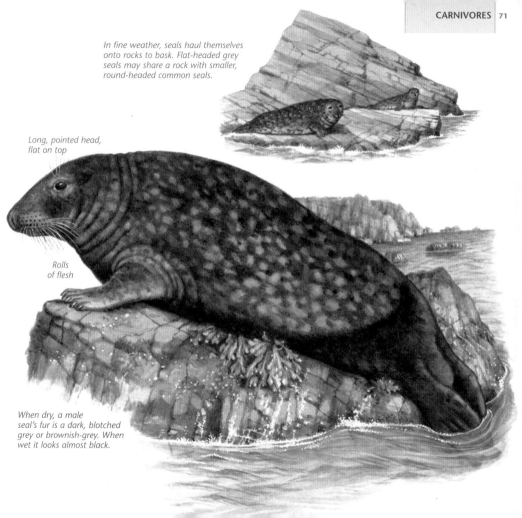

In fine weather, seals haul themselves onto rocks to bask. Flat-headed grey seals may share a rock with smaller, round-headed common seals.

Long, pointed head, flat on top

Rolls of flesh

When dry, a male seal's fur is a dark, blotched grey or brownish-grey. When wet it looks almost black.

A grey seal colony

IN THE WET, misty days of autumn grey seals come ashore to their breeding grounds on rocky islands or lonely beaches – normally to the same place year after year. The big bulls arrive first to establish territories above the high-tide line. The biggest bulls, the beachmasters, have the most extensive territories and the largest harems – about ten or more cows – so they father the greatest number of next season's pups.

The cows come ashore a few days after the bulls and are ready to give birth from the previous season's mating. They join a harem, not necessarily with the same bull every year, and are jealously guarded while they have their single pup because they are ready for mating

Scavenging skuas patrol the breeding beaches looking for dead and sickly pups. These birds also feed on the afterbirth.

3 *A cow returning from feeding finds her own pup by first recognising the place, then picking out its voice and finally by sniffing the pup to check its scent.*

1 *If the breeding beaches get overcrowded, some cows are driven inland.*

2 *A pup sheds its long, creamy-white baby coat after two or three weeks and becomes pale grey. At five weeks old it is ready to go to sea.*

soon after giving birth. Implantation of the fertilised egg is delayed for about three months so that a cow will not give birth before the following autumn.

Once the pups are weaned and leave the breeding beaches, they do not return for several years until they are adult. Cows mature at four or five years old, then come ashore to breed every year until they are about 35 or more. Bulls may mature at about six years old but are not big enough or strong enough to gain and defend a territory until they are at least nine. They then breed every year for about four or five seasons, but become worn out with the strain. Few males survive beyond about 20 years old.

4 *A cow defends the area around her own pup and fiercely repels intruders, including other pups, with bared teeth, hoots and threatening lunges. Some pups become lost or are abandoned.*

5 *Late-arriving bulls may challenge beachmasters for possession in noisy contests of strength. Often they fail to secure a patch and are forced to stay on the fringe of the colony or in the shallows.*

6 *A cow bears one pup, which feeds on her rich milk every 5 hours for three weeks. During this time the pup triples its 14kg birth weight, but the cow cannot go to sea to feed.*

7 *After her pup is three weeks old, a cow goes to feed as the tide rises. A bull dare not desert his territory, so lives off his fat reserves for nearly eight weeks.*

EXMOOR PONY

PONIES HAVE PROBABLY lived on Exmoor since about 60,000 BC, long before the last Ice Age ended. Today's ponies are hardy and well equipped to survive cold and wet, living outdoors through the worst weather. The thick, wiry coat covers a dense undercoat that insulates the body so well that in winter ponies often have unmelted snow on their backs, and their roomy nostrils have a large surface of skin that warms up the air before it enters the lungs. The deep jaws of the ponies have strong, deeply rooted teeth for dealing with the tough moorland grass.

Exmoor ponies also have great strength and endurance. Although small, they can carry a 12 stone (75kg) man all day, and are used as mounts by Devon shepherds.

The tail and mane are thick. Around the tail root the hairs form a 'thatch' that sheds the rain.

A distinct fleshy ridge over the eye (known as toad eye) deflects the rain.

The face is broad with a wide forehead, short, thick ears, a deep jaw and broad, black nostrils.

Foals are born between March and November, with most births about April. Short manes and tails reach adult length after about two years.

Exmoor pony
Equus (domestic)
200cm long; 130cm to shoulder
Half-wild herds on Exmoor, but many domesticated ponies throughout Britain.

The common colours are dun, bay and brown, all with distinctive oatmeal colouring round the eye and on the muzzle and underparts. Noted for its stamina and hardiness, the pony has strong, wiry hairs that shed the rain. The whorl-patterning of the hair on its flank throws the rain off on each side, away from the crease of the groin.

Broad chest and broad, level back

Strong, stocky build

Short legs

New Forest pony

Wild ponies have roamed the New Forest in Hampshire since Saxon times, and half-wild herds still remain. The ponies may be any colour except piebald and skewbald. There are two types: lightly built ponies up to 13.2 hands (137cm) high at the withers, and heavier-built ponies up to 14.2 hands (147cm).

DARTMOOR PONY

SMALL AND STURDY Dartmoor ponies make excellent riding ponies. Many run wild on their native Dartmoor and are rounded up yearly in autumn by their owners for branding. Suitable ones are kept for selling, others are returned to the moor for breeding. The ponies are hardy enough to withstand the worst of Dartmoor's winter weather, scratching through the snow to find food. Cattle grids on access roads confine the animals to the moor.

Because there is no restriction on the breed of stallion that can be turned out on the moor, few of the hardy moorland ponies are pure-bred. At one time Shetland stallions were introduced by miners in order to breed pit ponies. Today most pure-bred Dartmoor ponies are kept in private studs and are no longer hardy enough to winter on the moor. The maximum standard height set for the pony is 12.2 hands (127cm) at the withers.

1 *Its strong legs, tough feet and sturdy body enable the Dartmoor pony to survive on the moor's rock-strewn slopes and amid its numerous bogs. When foraging for bog grasses, ponies may sink belly deep into the soft ground.*

2 *Breeding herds of Dartmoor ponies run free on the moor. They are led by a stallion who keeps together a number of mares and foals, a herd ranging from about 5 up to 30. The ponies can live around 25 years.*

5 Ponies spend most of their time grazing, each herd within its own territory, and will travel many miles in search of food. As well as moor grasses, sedges and rushes, the ponies will eat heather and even gorse if no other food is available.

6 Most Dartmoor ponies are bay, brown or black. A few are grey or chestnut. The thick mane and long tail help to protect them from rain, and in August they start to grow a thicker coat that remains until May.

3 The stallion is ever watchful for danger, rivals or straying mares. Stragglers are chased and soundly nipped. When his own filly (female) foals are about two years old, they are driven off to join another herd.

4 Starlings are often seen among a herd of ponies. The flies that gather round the ponies provide the birds with a rich food supply.

RED DEER

SCOTLAND IS THE STRONGHOLD of Britain's wild red deer – the largest of our native animals. There are probably more than a quarter of a million red deer in the Highlands and Islands. Most other wild herds are on Exmoor and in the Quantock Hills, the New Forest, Thetford Forest and the Lake District.

Except at rutting time in autumn, the stags (males) live in separate groups from the hinds (females). Deer in woodland live in small groups, perhaps resting and ruminating by day and then grazing at night. Highland deer are usually seen in larger herds, moving up the hillsides by day to feed on grasses, heather and lichens and sheltering in the deeper heather or woods at night. In summer they usually keep to the higher hill slopes, following the growth of new heather. In winter they move to lower ground. The red deer's bright summer coat changes to a thicker grey-brown from about September to May. Although Highland deer are hardy and can scrape through snow to find food, many die in severe weather. The farming of red deer for venison has become widespread.

The deer use either their feet or antlers to scratch when irritated by parasites. Stags grow new antlers in summer. Antlers are full-grown and hard by September.

Hinds are slightly smaller than stags, and lack antlers. A deer grooms its coat by licking it and combing it with the front teeth of the lower jaw.

Calves are born singly, most in late May or June. A hind cleans under her calf's tail as she suckles it. The calf lies hidden in the undergrowth for much of the first week or so of its life. Calves are brown with white spots.

Red deer

Cervus elaphus

Stag 200cm long; 120cm to shoulder

Biggest wild herds found in Scotland, Devon, New Forest and Cumbria. Common in parks.

Family groups comprising a hind, her calf and a yearling born the previous summer are frequently seen together. The deer are often active at dawn and dusk.

Many-tined antlers

Buff-coloured rump and short tail

Britain's native red deer takes its name from the bright red-brown of its summer coat. Mature stags have antlers with many points (tines). Antlers can grow to about 70cm long.

For most of the year the stags live in separate groups from the hinds, yearlings and calves. In September the stags split up, each stag seeking out the hinds to try gathering a harem.

Rival stags often walk beside each other, slowly and some way apart, while they assess each other's strength. One may walk away, but if they appear to be evenly matched they will begin to fight.

Rutting stags emit deep, bellowing roars. Rivals try to outdo each other's roaring. They assess each other from the performance before they commit themselves to a fight.

Stags at war

FOR THREE WEEKS from early September the countryside echoes to the bellowing roars and the clashing of antlers of red deer stags. This is the rutting season, the courting and mating time when the stags move into the areas where the hinds live. Stags are now in their prime, with hard, fully grown antlers, a thick neck, a heavy winter mane and plenty of fat reserves built up during the rich summer's grazing.

Each stag tries to round up a harem of hinds, but his success depends on his size, age and how impressive he looks to other stags. The more he is threatened by rivals, the more he displays his strength by bellowing or thrashing trees with his antlers. Although intense fights occur between evenly matched animals, most contests are settled by a display of strength. The most successful stags are those about eight years old, who may hold harems of 10-20 hinds. Rutting stags use up a huge amount of energy, so often emerge from the rut thin and exhausted.

A stag will wallow in mud soaked with urine until its body is mud-plastered. This helps to spread the strong rutting smell all over its body.

As each hind in the harem becomes ready for mating, she emits a scent that attracts the stag, which may chase and sniff her.

Before mating, the stag licks and nuzzles the hind. A southern hind is usually two years old when she has her first calf; a hind in the harsher Highlands may be three or four.

Stags fight with a furious clashing of antlers as each tries to push away the other. Injuries or broken antlers may result, but fights to the death are rare. Very occasionally two stags cannot unlock their antlers and both die.

FALLOW DEER

WILD HERDS of fallow deer have lived for centuries in ancient forests such as Epping Forest and the Forest of Dean. They were a favourite quarry of medieval huntsmen, and later graced the parks of stately homes. Animals that escaped from parks have now established many feral herds.

The fallow is unusual among deer because there are several colour varieties. Chestnut-brown with white spots is the typical summer colouring, but some animals, known as menil, are pale brown with spots, and there are intermediates between the two as well as both black and white varieties. Park herds may be all one colour but in the wild mixed herds are more usual.

Fawns are born singly in June, hidden in long grass or bracken. Black fawns have brownish dappling. Typical colouring is chestnut-brown with white spots. Unspotted sandy fawns grow up to be white animals.

Menil fawns are pale brown with white spots. All menil fallow deer have brown markings on the back, rump and tail.

At rutting time – the October to November mating period – rival bucks fight fiercely, often clashing antlers. A buck's neck will be enlarged and his Adam's apple even more conspicuous. He utters loud, bellowing eerie groans.

Fallow deer

Dama dama

150cm long; 95cm to shoulder

Most wild herds in south and east. Common in parks.

Even in bucks of the same age, antlers vary in size and shape. The three bucks shown are all in their fourth year. A mature buck has antlers up to about 50cm long.

Broad-bladed antlers

Black-bordered rump and long, black, white-fringed tail

Prominent Adam's apple

Fallow does have no antlers. They, and bucks, may be seen feeding at any time, but dawn and dusk are generally favoured in the wild. By day they rest and ruminate in undergrowth or undisturbed pasture.

Typical summer coat

Fallow deer in summer

A DEER PARK is one of the best places to see fallow deer, especially on evenings in late June when most fawns are old enough to gambol. Fawns spend much of the day trotting after their mothers and grazing, but are suckled several times a day.

The bucks cast their antlers from late March to early June. They spend summer in a bachelor group while new antlers are developing. When the antlers are fully grown – towards the end of August for older bucks – the soft covering, or velvet,

is cleaned off by rubbing them against trees until they are clean and hard, ready for rutting in autumn.

From two years a doe usually bears a fawn every year for perhaps ten years or more, and herds increase rapidly. To prevent overcrowding, disease and destruction of their habitat, the deer are regularly culled (selectively killed); bucks from August to April, does from November to February.

1 *Grazing females keep a watchful eye on their fawns playing nearby. The deer constantly flick their tails to brush away flies.*

2 *Animals of different colour varieties interbreed. A fawn is not necessarily the same colour as either parent.*

6 The bucks live peaceably together in summer, separate from the does and fawns. They put on weight as they graze on the rich grass, and are in their prime in August and September – the 'fat buck' season.

7 Trees have a distinct browse line at about 1.5-2m – the height the deer can reach to feed when standing on hind legs.

8 Young trees are protected by wooden or metal cradles to prevent deer browsing on shoots and stripping bark.

3 Most fawns are born about mid June, and by the end of June are two or three weeks old. They sometimes play in groups, chasing each other and jumping on and off grassy hillocks.

4 Late-born fawns may be seen resting in the grass while others play. All fawns rest for much of the day in the first week or two of life.

5 Deer seem to enjoy the taste of a salt lick, fixed to a tree or stump. It provides them with minerals such as sodium, calcium and magnesium.

SIKA DEER

UNLIKE ITS CLOSE relative the red deer, the sika deer is not native to Britain but was introduced about 150 years ago to a number of deer parks. It originates from parts of eastern Asia, including China and Japan, where it is known as the spotted deer. Feral herds in parts of Britain are derived from escaped or released animals. Because of their close relationship, sika and red deer will interbreed and produce fertile hybrid offspring.

Sika deer are most active at dawn and dusk, when they leave the undergrowth to graze. Rutting takes place from late September to early November. Mature males (stags) mark out their territories by thrashing bushes and fraying tree bark with their antlers, and fight off rivals to gather a harem of females (hinds). Their call is a distinctive loud whistle repeated several times.

The hind is slightly smaller than the stag. In winter the coat is greyish-brown and the white rump prominent. Hock glands stand out as raised cushions on the hind legs.

Calves are born in May and June, with white spots that disappear after a few months.

If one or both rival stags have cast their antlers (in April or May), they settle a dispute by boxing instead of clashing antlers.

Sika deer

Cervus nippon

140cm long;
80cm to shoulder

Distribution patchy. Herds in wild are all derived from escaped or released animals.

When alarmed, a sika deer flares its rump hairs.

Rounded ears

In summer the coat is a bright chestnut-brown. Lighter hair on the forehead darkens at the brow to give a frowning look.

When first alerted to danger, a sika will turn to face the disturbance before deciding whether or not to run away.

White tail, often with a dark stripe, and white rump with dark edging

REINDEER

Short grasses, sedges and lichens are the reindeer's main food. In winter they scrape away snow to expose lichens. In spring they eat willow and birch shoots.

ABOUT 200,000 YEARS AGO reindeer were numerous in Britain, and the icy landscape must have resounded to the noise of thousands of clicking hoofs as herds migrated between summer and winter feeding grounds. The herds dwindled, perhaps as the climate changed, and the last survivors lived in Scotland. No one knows for certain when they finally died out. Reindeer were re-introduced to Scotland in 1952, when a domesticated Swedish herd from Lapland was released in the Cairngorm mountains near Aviemore.

In summer, male reindeer (bulls) are usually solitary, joining the herds of females (cows) and young animals for the September-October rut (mating season). After the rut, the bulls separate from the herd but follow it. Cows grow antlers,

Bulls have larger antlers than cows. Old bulls cast their antlers soon after the September-October rut and grow new ones in winter. Young bulls keep antlers for a few months after the rut.

the only female deer to do so. Although mature bulls shed their antlers in autumn, the cows carry theirs until spring. In winter, the cows can use their antlers to defend feeding patches cleared for themselves and their calves.

The coat colour varies widely, but many animals are greyish or brownish. The thick winter coat is paler. In late summer bulls grow a mane of white hair that persists throughout winter.

Long, sweeping antlers with flattened main branches and points, and forward-pointing branches with secondary branches.

A reindeer's broad, cloven hoofs are splayed to spread its weight and avoid sinking too deep in snow. The hoofs make a clicking sound as it walks.

Calves begin to develop antler pedicles (stalks) at about two months old. The antlers are fully grown before winter ends.

Reindeer

Rangifer tarandus

200cm long;
120cm to shoulder

Herd near Aviemore in Cairngorms, Scotland.

Calves are born in May or June, and, unlike most other deer, have no spots. They can walk within an hour.

ROE DEER

IN THE MIDDLE AGES the roe deer, the smallest native deer, was widespread in Britain. Later it gradually disappeared, surviving in only a few places. About 100 years ago the deer was restored to parts of England and has spread to many woodland and upland areas.

Roe deer generally keep to cover, and are usually seen in small groups or singly. They are most active at dawn and dusk and feed mainly on tree shoots or shrubs. Rutting, or mating, takes place in July and August. A male (buck) establishes his territory at the end of May, when his antlers are fully grown. He rubs against bushes and trees to scent them and barks at and chases rival bucks. Females (does) who enter the territory are then courted and mated. Roe deer are the only hoofed mammals in which implantation of the fertilised egg is delayed. It does not occur until December and the young are born the following May or June. Twins are common and sometimes triplets are born.

The kids are spotted with white. The spots gradually fade and after two months disappear. A doe may lie down to suckle a newborn kid. For its first few days a kid hides in vegetation, the doe visiting it at intervals.

Buck

Doe

Roe deer have short tails. The rump patch is white in winter. Does do not have antlers

Roe deer

Capreolus capreolus

120cm long;
64cm to shoulder

Forest deer spreading in many areas, especially to new plantations.

Antlers are cast in November or December. During winter new ones grow, protected from frost by a woolly skin (velvet) rubbed off by May.

Large ears, furry inside

Black nose

White chin patch

Buff rump

A roe deer's summer coat is a sleek, foxy red. A buck's antlers are roughened (pearled) near the base.

The grey-brown winter coat that grows in September and October is moulted in the following spring. The deer look scruffy while the winter coat is moulting. A wary deer will often stamp a foot.

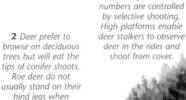

3 As deer have few natural predators, numbers are controlled by selective shooting. High platforms enable deer stalkers to observe deer in the rides and shoot from cover.

2 Deer prefer to browse on deciduous trees but will eat the tips of conifer shoots. Roe deer do not usually stand on their hind legs when browsing.

1 In April roe deer clean the velvet from their fully grown antlers by rubbing against trees. Branches may be broken and the bark rubbed off. Red deer do the same thing in August.

4 All deer like to browse on the brambles that grow in clearings. Roe deer are especially fond of them.

Deer in the forest

ROE DEER are particularly numerous in the coniferous forests of northern Britain, but are shy creatures that will disappear into the trees if disturbed. They are most likely to be spotted as they cross a forest ride. At about two years old a roe buck acquires a territory that he normally occupies for life. The size of the territory varies, and may cover about 5-30ha (12-75 acres). During spring and summer, the buck patrols the boundary of his territory, marking it by rubbing scent from his head glands against trees and fighting with any intruding bucks. Roe deer females also have territories, but do not defend them. Their

5 A roe buck disturbed as it browses will bound into the cover of the trees. It may clear about 5m in one leap.

6 Fallow deer come to graze in the grassy forest rides – the broad paths between stands of trees. Fallow of various colours, muntjac, roe and red deer may all be found in one forest.

7 Creatures of habit, deer regularly take the same route through the forest, making well-trodden paths.

territories often overlap with those of other does and several bucks.

Deer of any species may cause considerable damage to trees by fraying bark when they clean their antlers, by breaking branches when they thrash with their antlers at rutting time and also by stripping bark to eat. A tree's growth may be distorted, and if bark is rubbed or stripped off all round, the tree will die. Deer also browse on accessible shoots, large deer reaching as high as 1.8-2.1m when standing on their hind legs. In commercial forests the damage can be serious, and new plantations in traditional red deer areas are generally fenced off.

MUNTJAC

ALTHOUGH IT IS CALLED the barking deer in its native Asia, the muntjac is one of several deer species in Britain that barks. The Chinese, or Reeves's, muntjac was introduced to the Duke of Bedford's Woburn estate in Bedfordshire in 1894. Since then the descendants of escaped or released animals have become established in England, and are still spreading thanks to the ability of the females (does) to conceive a few days after fawning and give birth every seven months. Unlike native deer, they have no fixed breeding season.

When alarmed, a muntjac lifts its tail to show the white underside – maybe to warn other deer as it runs away.

Muntjac are active by day or night but most often at dusk, feeding on grass, brambles and other plants, such as ivy and yew. Their winter coats are duller and thicker than their summer coats. Like all deer, muntjac have scent glands that help them to communicate with each other. To mark territory they rub their heads against the ground or a tree to leave scent. A male (buck) establishes a territory that includes the home area of several does and will fight rival bucks. He uses his fine-pointed fang-like teeth as weapons.

Muntjac fawns are born singly at any time of the year. Their spotted coats make them hard to see in the undergrowth. By the time they are eight weeks old the spots have faded.

Muntjac

Muntiacus reevesi

100cm long; 48cm to shoulder

Found in woodland and scrub. Introduced to Bedfordshire, still rapidly spreading.

Short antlers

Rounded back

A muntjac's tongue is extremely mobile and so long it can reach to lick the corner of its eye. A buck has a V-shaped ridge on the forehead, extending down from his antlers and marked by dark stripes.

Buck has fang-like teeth in upper jaw.

White-edged tail

The smallest British deer, the muntjac has a glossy, red-brown summer coat and is distinguished by its rounded back and white-edged tail. A doe lacks antlers and has a black triangular patch on her forehead.

A buck's short antlers are cast in May or June and grow again in summer. A muntjac has large glands below the eye, in pits almost as big as the eye socket.

CHINESE WATER DEER

THE REED SWAMPS and grassy river valleys of north-east China are the original home of the Chinese water deer. It was introduced to England at Woburn Park, Bedfordshire, in the early 20th century. Animals bred there were supplied to Whipsnade Park, and in turn were sent to parks in various counties. Some deer escaped, but few feral populations have become established, although a number have flourished in the Cambridgeshire fens and the Broads of East Anglia, where wetlands with dense reed beds and clumps of alder provide thick cover.

Feral water deer are usually solitary or in small groups. In contrast, deer in parks gather in large groups and are easily seen, particularly at Whipsnade, where many range freely through the park or run over the Downs, leaping and bounding through the grass with hind legs flung high. Large numbers often gather on the surrounding fields, especially during the November and December rutting season. They bark, whicker and squeak as they chase one another.

The deer feed mainly on grasses, rarely browsing on shrubs or trees. Does are slightly smaller than bucks.

The tail is short and held close to the rump. It is inconspicuous, especially in winter when the deer's coat is pale grey-brown and thick.

Chinese water deer

Hydropotes inermis

100cm long; 60cm to shoulder

Feral groups in and around Bedfordshire, also Broads and Fens. Park herds elsewhere.

Large rounded ears,
furry on the inside

The Chinese water deer
is the only deer in Britain
where the male has no
antlers. The deer is slightly
higher at the haunch
than at the shoulder,
and in summer is a
sleek red-brown.

Tusk-like
teeth in
male

Fawns are born about June
and are spotted. Twins and
triplets are usual, but sextuplets
may occur. Many fawns die
soon after birth.

As with other
ruminants, a period
of grazing is followed
by a period of rest,
during which the
deer chews the cud.

AXIS DEER

NATIVE TO INDIA and Sri Lanka, the spotted axis deer can be seen in some zoos, and deer parks such as those at Woburn and Whipsnade, both in Bedfordshire. Axis is said to be the name that was given it by the Roman administrator Pliny the Elder in his *Natural History*, written in the 1st century AD.

In its homelands, the axis deer lives mainly in lowland forest areas where there is good cover as well as good grazing. It also ventures from the forest to feed on the crops of nearby villages, and this has led to many deer being killed. Early last century herds could be reckoned in their thousands, but now there are far fewer.

As with most deer, axis deer graze by day or night, or browse on shrubs. When alarmed, they emit a shrill whistle. There is no set breeding season, and young calves may be seen in parks at any time of the year. Nor is there a fixed season for stags (males) to shed their antlers, so all stages of antler growth, as well as hard antlers cleaned of velvet, can be seen at any time.

Three-tined antlers

White bib

The axis deer's summer coat is rich brown heavily dappled with white spots. Winter colouring is slightly darker. A stag's three-tined (pointed) antlers can grow up to 76cm.

A well-grown axis fawn resembles a fallow deer. It can be distinguished by its white bib.

Axis deer

Axis axis

120cm long;
95cm to shoulder

A forest species in the wild. In Britain seen at Woburn and some other parks and zoos.

PÈRE DAVID'S DEER

Backswept points

Squarish muzzle

In summer the coat of the Père David's deer is tawny red flecked with grey; in winter it is longer and greyish-buff.

Long tail

Large feet that click like a reindeer's

NO ONE KNOWS how the Père David's deer behaves in its wild state, because by the time it was first described to zoologists in 1865 it was probably already extinct in the wild. A French missionary and explorer, Père Armand David, discovered a herd in the walled Imperial Hunting Park near Peking (Beijing) in China, and some were exported to Europe. This was fortunate because the Peking herd was killed off – by flooding, by hungry peasants and during the Boxer war around 1900. The 11th Duke of Bedford, who had been sent a pair of the deer from France, acquired all those still alive in Europe and began to breed the deer on his Woburn estate in Bedfordshire. There they thrived, and from the Woburn herd Père David's deer have been sent to zoos throughout the world, and to reserves in their native China. A large deer, like the reindeer, Père David's has a rounded, horse-like rump and unusually shaped antlers, which re-grow in winter. The stags fight during the rut in July and August as each tries to keep his harem of hinds (females).

Père David's deer

Elaphurus davidianus

190cm long;
120cm to shoulder

Can be seen in Woburn park, Bedfordshire, and some other safari and zoological parks.

Calves are born between March and May. They have spotted coats and the leggy look of a foal.

A stag will festoon its antlers with vegetation during the rutting season. Hinds have no antlers.

SMALL RED-BROWN DEER WITHOUT ANTLERS

Muntjac doe
Muntiacus reevesi
Dark patch on forehead.
Plain muzzle. Back often
rounded. Tail inconspicuous
but shows white below
when raised in alarm.
Shoulder height 48cm.
Page 94

Roe doe
Capreolus capreolus
Black muzzle, white chin.
Creamy-buff rump; no
visible tail, but has a
hanging tuft of hair.
Shoulder height 64cm.
Page 90

Chinese water doe or buck
Hydropotes inermis
Large, round ears. Black nose. Plain
rump. Buck has two protruding, tusk-like
teeth. Shoulder height 60cm. Page 96

Deer in summer

ONCE THEY HAVE moulted their winter coats –
usually by May or June, depending on the
species and the weather – deer have bright,
glossy summer coats. Several species are similar
in colour and build. The main identification
points are the variations in rump pattern, tail
markings and length and, in males, the shape
of the antlers. Within a species, both antler
shapes and shoulder heights, which are given
as a guide to species size, can vary with age
and among individuals of the same age.

SMALL RED-BROWN DEER WITH SHORT ANTLERS

Roe buck
Capreolus capreolus
Antlers clean, no velvet.
Black muzzle, white
chin. Creamy-buff
rump, no visible tail.
Shoulder height 66cm.
Page 90

Muntjac buck
Muntiacus reevesi
Antlers with velvet. Dark face stripes. Plain
muzzle. Rump plain but shows white when tail
lifted in alarm. Shoulder height 48cm. Page 94

SPOTTED DEER WITH ANTLERS

Sika stag
Cervus nippon
Antlers with several
points. Black lip patch.
White tail, often with
dark stripe.
White rump
with dark
edging.
Shoulder
height 80cm.
Page 86

Fallow
buck of
typical colour
Dama dama
Antlers with several
points and broad
blades. Plain lip.
Long, dark, white-
fringed tail. White
rump with black
border. Shoulder
height 95cm. Page 82

Young red deer stag
Cervus elaphus
Occasionally lightly spotted. Antlers with
several points. Black lip patch. Buff rump.
Shoulder height 114cm. Page 78

SPOTTED DEER WITHOUT ANTLERS

Red deer calf a
few months old
Cervus elaphus
Black lip patch.
Fading spots. Buff
rump. Shoulder
height under
76cm. Page 78

Fallow doe of
typical colour
Dama dama
No lip patch. Long,
black, white-fringed
tail. White rump
with black border.
Shoulder height 76cm.
Page 82

Sika hind *Cervus nippon*
Black lip patch. White tail, often
with a dark stripe. White rump
with dark edging. Shoulder
height 70cm. Page 86

GREYISH-BROWN OR BROWN DEER WITHOUT ANTLERS

Roe doe
Capreolus capreolus
Black muzzle. White rump
patch with a short tuft
of hairs hanging down.
Shoulder height 64cm.
Page 90

Red stag without
antlers (hummel)
Cervus elaphus
A mature male able to breed
although it has failed to grow
antlers. Heavy mane on neck.
Black lip patch. Buff rump.
Shoulder height
117cm. Page 78

Fallow doe of
typical colour
Dama dama
Long, black, white-fringed
tail. White rump with
black border. Shoulder
height 76cm. Page 82

Black fallow doe
Dama dama
Long black tail; tip may
be copper-coloured. No
white on rump. Shoulder
height 76cm. Page 82

Deer in winter

WINTER COATS usually start growing about
September and are duller and thicker than
summer coats. Species with spots in
summer generally lose them in winter.
Most young deer change to adult colouring
at a few months old. As in summer, the key
identification points are the variations in
rump pattern, tail markings and length
and, in males, antler shapes. Shoulder
heights are given as a guide to species size,
but vary with age and among individuals.

Muntjac doe
Muntiacus reevesi
Back often rounded. Plain rump.
Tail inconspicuous but shows
white below when raised.
Shoulder height 48cm. Page 94

Red hind
Cervus elaphus
Black lip patch. Buff
rump. Shoulder height
114cm. Page 78

Sika hind
Cervus nippon
White tail, often with a dark stripe.
White rump with dark edging.
Shoulder height 70cm. Page 86

GREYISH-BROWN OR BROWN DEER WITH LARGE ANTLERS

Red stag
Cervus elaphus
Antlers with many
points and two low
forward branches.
Buff rump. Shoulder
height 120cm.
Page 78

Young
red stag
Cervus elaphus
Antlers with several
points. Buff rump.
Shoulder height
110cm. Page 78

Sika stag
Cervus nippon
Antlers with several points.
White tail, often with dark stripe.
White rump with dark
edging. Shoulder
height 80cm.
Page 86

Fallow buck of
typical colour
Dama dama
Antlers with several
points and broad blades.
Long, dark, white-fringed
tail. White rump with
black border. Shoulder
height 95cm. Page 82

Young black
fallow buck
Dama dama
Antlers with several points but
blades not yet broad. Long dark
tail; tip may be copper-coloured.
Shoulder height 89cm. Page 82

GREYISH-BROWN OR BROWN DEER WITH SHORT ANTLERS

Young sika stag
with first antlers
Cervus nippon
Antlers clean,
no velvet. White
rump with hairs
fluffed as alarm
signal. Plain
muzzle. Shoulder
height 70cm.
Page 86

Muntjac buck
Muntiacus reevesi
Antlers clean, no velvet (except on
immature bucks). Inconspicuous
rump, shows white when tail lifted
in alarm. Dark stripes on face.
Muzzle plain. Shoulder
height 48cm.
Page 94

Roe buck
Capreolus capreolus
Antlers with velvet. White
rump with hairs fluffed as
alarm signal. Black muzzle.
Shoulder height 66cm.
Page 90

Antlers

ONLY DEER GROW ANTLERS, which are quite different from horns, though they are used similarly – mainly as weapons. Horns are permanent bony growths covered with a sleeve of horn, and occur in both sexes. Antlers are bony growths that drop off and regrow every year; except for reindeer, only males grow them. While antlers grow they are covered by a hairy skin called velvet. Blood vessels in the velvet supply food and oxygen to the growing bone. When the antler is fully grown the velvet is shed or rubbed off and the antler dies, though it stays on the deer's head for several months.

The antler cycle is similar in all deer, but times of casting and cleaning differ. Most species in Britain shed antlers in early spring or summer and have new ones fully grown in late summer or autumn, before rutting time. Roe deer shed antlers in winter and have fully grown ones about April. With some deer, each pair of antlers is normally larger and with more tines, or points, than the previous pair until the deer reaches old age. The number of points can indicate if a deer is young or old.

THE ANTLER CYCLE OF A FALLOW DEER

FIRST YEAR

March

May

1 Growth begins
Early in the year after its birth, a male fallow fawn grows pedicles, or stalks, for its antlers.

2 Antlers appear
Soon the pedicles bear small antlers covered with a hairy skin called velvet.

Mid May

3 First pair growing
Growth is rapid, but size varies. The first set may be short stubs or slender spikes. Rarely, they may have one or two branches.

Late July

Mid August

4 Growth complete
When the antlers are fully grown, the velvet dries and shrivels. The buck rubs it off against a tree.

5 Antlers clean and hard
When all the velvet has been cleaned off, the antlers die but stay on the pedicles until late the following spring.

SECOND YEAR

Late
May

6 Antlers cast
The antlers are cast, or shed, one at a time. The second antler may be cast a few days after the first.

Late
May

7 Scabs form
When an antler is cast, blood oozes slightly from the pedicle, then dries up and a scab begins to form.

Mid
June

8 New growth begins
Two weeks later the antlers are growing fast, and show clearly above the pedicles.

Early
July

9 Branches form
Soon each antler branches into a brow tine, pointing forwards, and a main beam, pointing backwards.

Late
July

10 More tines appear
The antlers grow rapidly, and more tines (or points) branch off the main beam.

Late
August

11 Growth complete
A month later the antlers are fully grown but are still covered in velvet.

Late
August

12 Velvet shed
As the velvet is shed and rubbed off, the antlers are untidy and blood-stained for several days.

End of
August

13 Antlers clean
A few days later all the velvet is gone and the antlers are clean and hard. In the following spring the cycle begins again.

FERAL GOAT

STONE AGE FARMERS brought goats to Britain, and there have been herds of feral goats – descendants of domestic animals gone wild – in mountainous areas for more than 1,000 years. Shaggy feral goats were commoner than sheep in many places 200 years ago, but today herds are small and isolated. Colour and size varies much between goats, and because isolation prevents inter-breeding, those in one place tend to be different from those in another.

For most of the year the goats keep to high, rocky mountainsides or cliff tops, in winter descending to grassy valleys or farms in search of food. Towards the end of winter the herds disperse and females go off to give birth. At first a kid hides among boulders, visited by its mother two or three times a day. When about ten days old a kid is strong enough to follow its mother, and by summer females and youngsters have gathered into a herd. Many kids die of exposure, but adults are better able to withstand damp and drizzle, and often live for five years.

Sure-footed and agile, goats can forage on rocky slopes, and may be surprisingly hard to see.

Horns, which either sweep back or, more often, spread outwards, grow continually – a ram's can reach 76cm in length. The goat's long horns help to distinguish it from hill sheep, which have short, coiled horns.

Females tend to keep to one place, but males often range over many miles.

The young (kids) are born in January in the north, March or April in the south. One kid is usual, twins are uncommon.

Feral goat

Capra (domestic)

120cm long; 76cm to shoulder

Isolated herds in rocky areas of the north and west. Small herds on some islands.

Outward-spreading horns

The small, shaggy feral goat is a descendant of domestic goats of the past, before modern breeds were developed. Both sexes have horns.

Shaggy coat

Its shaggy coat distinguishes a feral goat from the larger modern, short-haired domestic goat.

The goats browse on shrubs such as gorse and heather, and will also eat leaves and shoots from trees. They sometimes stand on their hind legs to reach a branch.

SOAY SHEEP

TINY, DARK BROWN Soay sheep on the St Kilda islands in the Outer Hebrides are the only completely wild sheep in Britain. They are the kind of sheep kept centuries ago before selective breeding developed more productive animals, and would have died out but for their isolation on remote St Kilda. They supplied the islanders with wool and meat for hundreds of years until the last people left the islands in 1930.

Because the St Kilda sheep are no longer managed, the population tends to build up to more than 1,000. Then, because of overgrazing, as many as a third of them die of starvation at the end of winter. The population builds up again in the following three or four years to repeat the cycle.

The soay sheep's soft brown fleece is a popular choice for homespun garments. Because the sheep are not as heavy as domestic breeds, their hoofs do not cut into turf and encourage soil erosion. They are often kept on nature reserves where gentle grazing is needed to maintain short turf rich in orchids and other flowers.

The rams establish social dominance at rutting time by behaviour such as blocking – pushing against one another with one foot raised.

During the rutting season in late autumn, rams sniff with outstretched heads and necks as each one follows a ewe.

There are buff markings above each eye, and the pupils of the eyes are rectangular. On the ram's horns, dark annual growth rings can be seen between groups of ornamental ridges.

Soay sheep		
Ovis (domestic)		
90cm long; 55cm to shoulder		
Soay and Hirta islands in remote St Kilda group.		

Fawn coat

Pale underparts and rump

Slightly built Soay sheep resemble the primitive domestic sheep of Stone Age Britain. Ewes have small horns or none at all; rams have heavy, coiled horns. The fleece contains both wool and hair, and moults in June. St Kildans plucked the wool by hand – sheep were not shorn.

Dark brown coat

Soay lambs are born in mid April. Twins are not uncommon. Many lambs die at the end of winter when food is short.

In late summer the sheep population of St Kilda is at its peak; every few years there are so many that they eat all the available grass.

WILD BOAR

ONCE PART of our native wildlife, the wild boar became extinct in Britain in the late 1600s as a result of intensive hunting. For 300 years truly wild boar were unknown in Britain, but since the 1970s they have been escaping from captive herds and living in the wild. Today there are up to five breeding populations in the forests of Kent, East Sussex, Devon and Dorset, and in the Forest of Dean area.

Directly descended from the ancestors of domestic pigs, wild boar feed by rooting in the ground for nuts, acorns, roots, shoots, worms, insect larvae and other small animals. They are most active at twilight and by night, but boar that have recently escaped from captivity are less wary and often feed by day, often in small family groups. They have poor eyesight and rely on their ears and sense of smell to detect food and danger. They usually slip away if they feel threatened, but they have sharp tusks – especially the males – and can be dangerous if cornered.

In cold winters the soil freezes, making rooting for food impossible, and hungry wild boar may tear at dead and rotting timber to find wood-boring insect grubs and other small animals.

Wild boar regularly wallow in shallow pools or puddles in wet ground. This keeps them cool in summer, but the mud also helps to remove and discourage bloodsucking skin parasites such as mites and ticks.

Wild Boar

Sus scrofa

Length 130cm; tail 25cm

A few wild breeding colonies in the south.

Forest habitat

Although clearly pig-like in appearance, a wild boar looks very different from a typical domestic pig. Its head is much bigger compared to its relatively lean body, and it has powerful shoulders and slim hips. A male can weigh up to 200kg, but females are generally smaller, weighing up to 130kg. Both sexes have a thick coat of dark, bristly hair, with dense underfur in winter and a ridge of long bristles down the back.

Sensitive, hairless snout

Tasselled tail

Four toes

Male

Female

Mature males grow upward-pointing tusks from both their upper and lower jaws. The upper pair keep the lower pair sharp. Females do not have the upper tusks.

Solitary males frequently score the bark of trees with their sharp tusks to mark their territory.

After wallowing in mud, wild boar rub themselves against trees, leaving distinctive rubbing marks.

RED-NECKED WALLABY

KANGAROO-LIKE red-necked wallabies from the scrublands of Tasmania must be the most surprising creatures living free in our countryside. Many have escaped from zoos or wildlife parks, but only a few have survived to breed in the wild. The largest population, just a few dozen, lives in the Peak District National Park, descendants of wallabies that escaped from the grounds of a local mansion in about 1940. Another small population (now extinct) became established in Ashdown Forest in Sussex. There have also been reports of some in the Loch Lomond area.

Britain's few wild wallabies are shy and rarely seen. They are well suited to living in thickets and woods, and are used to the cool, wet climate of Tasmania, but harsh winters and deep snow cause many to die. The wallaby's chief hazards are probably disturbance by people and competition for food from large numbers of sheep.

When it bounds fast, the wallaby's long hind feet and long, thick tail are conspicuous. It uses only its hind legs, tucking the front legs up against its chest.

The wallaby can withstand moderately cool temperatures but is badly affected by very cold weather. In deep snow it struggles to move about and find food.

Heather is the wallaby's main food, especially in winter, but it also eats grass and bracken and browses on conifer seedlings and bilberry shoots. It sometimes uses its front feet to grasp plants.

Red-necked wallaby

Macropus rufogriseus

60cm; 64cm tail

Occurs in a small area of the Peak District and possibly around Loch Lomond. A few in Sussex have died out.

Red-brown
shoulder
patch

The shy red-necked wallaby tends
to hide in thick scrub. It takes its name
from the red-brown patch on its nape and
shoulders. Female slimmer than male.

Black-tipped feet

Black-tipped tail

The young
are born
singly at any
time of year.
A tiny new-
born wallaby
crawls up into its
mother's pouch and
attaches itself to a teat. It is
suckled for several months. Young
in the pouch are called joeys.

When a joey is a few months old it
begins to take solid food, and often
grazes from the pouch as its mother
bends forward to nibble the grass. A young wallaby
becomes independent from about 10 to 12 months old.

Young brown rat
Distinguished from mouse by feet larger and heavier in relation to body, and by thicker tail.

House mouse
Mus musculus
Head and body 83mm. Greasy fur and strong smell. Page 122

Broad yellow chest-band

Orange-coloured flanks

Yellow-necked mouse
Apodemus flavicollis
Head and body 10cm. Uncommon. Heavier than wood mouse. Page 128

Finely furred ears

Scaly tail

Juvenile wood mouse
Distinguished from house mouse by larger ears, longer hind feet and longer, thinner, hairy tail. Yellow mark on chest

Wood mouse
Apodemus sylvaticus
Head and body 95mm. Page 124

Brown rat
Rattus norvegicus
Head and body up to 28cm. Fur occasionally black. Page 116

Blunt nose

Yellow mark on chest

Tail shorter than head and body

Orange rump (adult)

Harvest mouse
Micromys minutus
Head and body 64mm. Uncommon. Tail used for grasping. Page 120

Identifying rats, mice, voles, shrews and dormice

TO TELL SMALL MAMMALS such as rats, voles and shrews apart, look at the shape of the nose, the size of the ears and the length of the tail in relation to the head and body. Colour and size alone can be deceptive.

Mice generally have pointed faces, big eyes, prominent ears and a long, thin tail usually longer than the head and body. Rats are like large, heavily built mice with coarse, shaggy fur and scaly tails. Voles are chubby and round-faced with short noses and fairly small eyes and ears. They have long, silky hair and their tails are comparatively short. Shrews are tiny and have long, narrow, pointed noses, small ears, pin-head size eyes and often quite hairy tails. Whereas voles and several species of mice have fur that is black at the base, shrews and dormice have fur that is all one colour.

Bank vole
Clethrionomys glareolus
Head and body 90mm. Adults red-brown, young greyer. Page 131

Ears clearly visible

Tail half as long as head and body

Water vole
Arvicola terrestris
Head and body 20cm. Heavily built. Round face. Fur occasionally black. Page 130

Orange fur on flanks

Field vole
Microtus agrestis
Head and body 10cm. Adults dark brown, young greyer. Page 133

Ears half hidden

Very short tail

Common shrew
Sorex araneus
Head and body 75mm. Page 174

Bulbous forehead

Grey belly with yellow tinge

Pygmy shrew
Sorex minutus
Head and body 64mm. Tiny. Page 176

Common dormouse
Muscardinus avellanarius
Head and body 75mm. Hairs similar colour from base to tip. Rare. Page 136

Big black eyes

Fluffy tail

White-toothed shrew
Crocidura russula (Greater)
Crocidura suaveolens (Lesser)

Head and body 60mm. Channel Isles and Isles of Scilly only. Page 180

Projecting hairs on tail

Prominent ears

Large pink ears

Tail longer than head and body

Black rat
Rattus rattus
Head and body 20cm. Slender build. Fur sometimes grey-brown. Rare. Page 118

White eyebrows and ear tips

Water shrew
Neomys fodiens
Head and body 86mm. Young grey-brown underneath. Uncommon. Page 178

Fringe on tail

BROWN RAT

A WIDESPREAD PEST, the brown rat fouls food stores and gnaws stored goods. It spread to Britain in the early 18th century, probably from Russia, and is found not only in buildings but also in many places outdoors, suchas rubbish tips and muddy shores where debris is washed up. Large numbers often build up on farms, where food is plentiful. In a fine summer, young rats may spread into hedgerows and lay-bys far from buildings. Brown rats are also at home in sewers, where they are especially liable to pick up and transmit diseases.

Where food and shelter are abundant, a female brown rat can produce five litters a year totalling 50 young, all able to breed at three months. But many young rats are caught by cats, owls, foxes and other predators. Rat numbers are also controlled by the use of poisons that prevent blood from clotting – although some rats have developed a resistance to them. The white rats of pet shops and laboratories are a specially bred form of brown rat.

A rat colony may be found among a pile of rubbish in a hedgerow. The rats live in under-ground burrows with trampled runways leading to them. Young rats emerge from the burrow at about three weeks old.

Brown rat

Rattus norvegicus

28cm

Common around buildings, in farms and hedgerows. Less usual on high ground, moors.

Often seen in the water, especially near a sewer, a swimming brown rat can be distinguished from a water vole by its pointed nose and greyer fur.

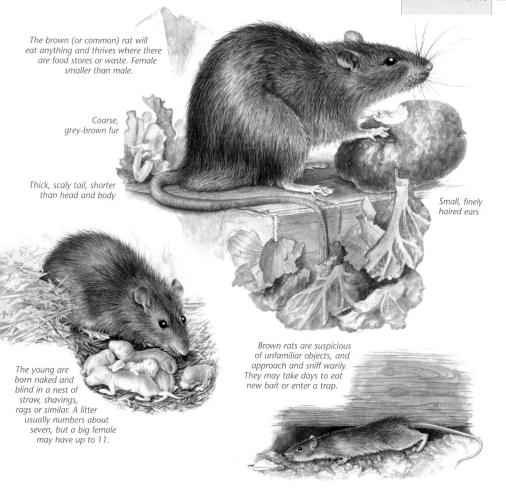

The brown (or common) rat will eat anything and thrives where there are food stores or waste. Female smaller than male.

Coarse, grey-brown fur

Thick, scaly tail, shorter than head and body

Small, finely haired ears

The young are born naked and blind in a nest of straw, shavings, rags or similar. A litter usually numbers about seven, but a big female may have up to 11.

Brown rats are suspicious of unfamiliar objects, and approach and sniff warily. They may take days to eat new bait or enter a trap.

BLACK RAT

WIDELY BLAMED for carrying plague, the black rat thrives in a man-made environment. The rat originated in tropical Asia, but spread to Europe as trade developed, reaching Britain probably in the 11th century. Plague was rife in Asia, the virus being transmitted by the rat flea. During the 14th century, a massive outbreak of disease that killed some 25 million people in Europe, including more than a third of Britain's population, was blamed on the rat flea. But modern research suggests that this may not have been rat-borne plague after all.

Because of its tropical origins, the black rat in Britain prefers to live in warm, sheltered buildings. Since the coming of the larger, more aggressive and adaptable brown rat some 300 years ago, the black rat has disappeared from most of its old haunts. It is now probably Britain's rarest mammal. Black rats usually have from three to five litters of six or seven young a year; they mature at about four months. Humans and domestic cats are their chief enemies.

Not all black rats are black. Brown forms can be distinguished from brown rats by their large pink ears and long tails. Brown varieties may have a grey or creamy-white belly.

The black rat wears down its constantly growing front teeth by gnawing, and may cause expensive damage to woodwork. It will even gnaw pipes and electric cables.

Black rat

Rattus rattus

20cm; 23cm tail

Almost extinct. Found mainly inside buildings, chiefly in major ports and old towns.

Its large eyes and ears and long whiskers help the black rat to find its way in dark buildings. It eats all sorts of food, but particularly cereals.

Large, bare
pink ears

Black rats are
active at night.
They climb easily up
a rope, brickwork or
even a thin strand
of wire. But, unlike
brown rats, they
are reluctant to
enter the water.

The black (or ship) rat
is mostly likely to be seen
in a dockside warehouse.
Female smaller than male.

Long thin tail, as
long as, or longer
than head and body.

The black rat
has greasy fur that
discolours a surface it often
rubs against. A rat hole gnawed
through wood can be recognised
by the stained edge.

HARVEST MOUSE

ONE OF THE world's smallest rodents, the harvest mouse weighs less than a 2p coin. Being so tiny it can climb fast and confidently among thin stalks. As their name implies, harvest mice have always been associated with cornfields, but now that these are reaped by machines and then ploughed up, they more often live in the long grass at the base of a hedge, invading the growing corn crop to nest and feed in early summer. Tall vegetation such as brambles and rushes is their main summer home, and they are common in reed beds. The peak breeding season is August and September. When young harvest mice become independent at about 16 days they are grey-brown, and later moult to adult colouring.

Urban development, hedge removal and the increase in intensive farming methods threaten harvest mice. But they may benefit from the huge areas of rank grass along motorway embankments. Active day and night, the mice are likely to be caught both by daytime and night-time predators – most live only a few months.

When tall plant stems die back in autumn, the harvest mice are left exposed and seek cover in low vegetation or sometimes in barns. Many mice die during winter.

In winter the mouse's coat is a darker brown. The winter nest is built low, usually in a clump of grass or under a hedge.

There are usually from three to eight young in a litter, born on a layer of chewed grass leaves. Females are pregnant for 17-19 days and may have three litters in a year, each in a new nest.

Harvest mouse

Micromys minutus

64mm; 64mm tail

Fairly widespread in coarse vegetation and hedgerows. Not found on high ground.

Blunt nose

Small ears

Yellow-brown fur

The tiny, agile harvest mouse lives among tall, stiff-stemmed vegetation and uses its tail as a fifth limb to grasp stalks.

Tail grasping stalk

Seeds, grain, grass shoots and soft fruit, as well as insects such as weevils, are all part of the harvest mouse's diet. Because it is very active, it has a large appetite for its size.

Breeding nests are built well off the ground, often in grass or reeds, and are spherical – about 90mm across. The framework is woven from neatly shredded living leaf blades, so the nest hangs between stems. Non-breeding nests are more loosely built.

HOUSE MOUSE

UNLIKE OTHER MICE, the house mouse has a strong smell and greasy fur. It taints the places it lives in – homes, warehouses, hospitals and other public buildings. Mice also leave their black droppings and their urine about, carry diseases and parasites, and cause damage by their gnawing. Although house mice live for only about 18 months, and many die in their first winter, it is hard for the humans they live with to get rid of them. They breed so fast that in one summer the mice from one nest will have multiplied many times over. Females bear from five to ten litters a year with five or six young in a litter. The young leave the nest at three weeks old and three weeks later the females among them are ready to breed.

House mice live close to their food supply and move on only when food is short. They are easily transported by accident among food or goods and, with the spread of humans, have colonised most of the Earth from their first home in Asia.

Male mice fight for social dominance or to defend territory, and any adult in a group may attack an outsider. Fighting increases as the population rises.

A mouse often sniffs with its nose raised. Its sense of smell is acute, and it can find its way about and recognise other family members by scent.

House mouse

Mus musculus

80mm; 80mm tail

Widespread, mostly in and around buildings, but also in hedgerows and on farmland.

When food is plentiful, house mice may live in fields and hedgerows in summer. Some may also move outdoors in late summer when indoor populations increase to high numbers. Few survive cold weather outdoors, so most winter in a building.

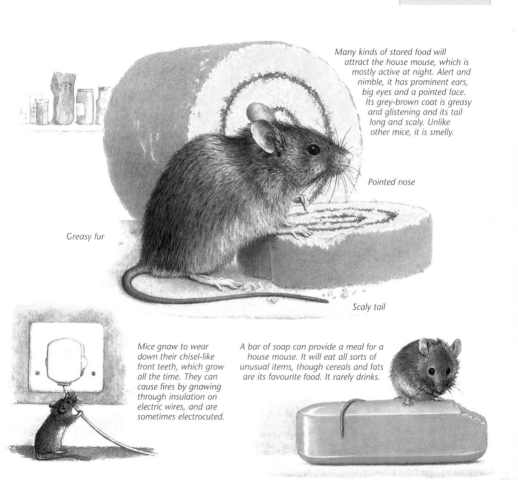

Many kinds of stored food will attract the house mouse, which is mostly active at night. Alert and nimble, it has prominent ears, big eyes and a pointed face. Its grey-brown coat is greasy and glistening and its tail long and scaly. Unlike other mice, it is smelly.

Pointed nose

Greasy fur

Scaly tail

Mice gnaw to wear down their chisel-like front teeth, which grow all the time. They can cause fires by gnawing through insulation on electric wires, and are sometimes electrocuted.

A bar of soap can provide a meal for a house mouse. It will eat all sorts of unusual items, though cereals and fats are its favourite food. It rarely drinks.

WOOD MOUSE

PROBABLY THE MOST widespread and abundant British mammal, the wood mouse – also known as the long-tailed field mouse – is not confined to woods. It thrives equally well in more open places, even on moors and mountain-sides, and is also common in gardens, where it often lives near sheds and outbuildings. Unlike house mice, wood mice do not smell strongly.

The wood mouse is very active, venturing into open places where other small mammals rarely go. Although it moves only under cover of darkness, it is often taken by predators, especially owls and cats. Most wood mice stay in the same general area but may travel more than 1km in one night. In winter they sometimes go into a torpid state – almost like hibernation – to conserve energy. This helps them to survive food shortages. The population is lowest at the end of winter, but numbers soon build up. Breeding starts in March, and a female may bear four litters a year, each of about five young. Wood mice are short-lived; the lifespan in the wild is rarely more than a year.

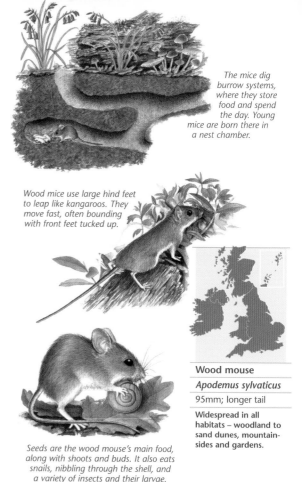

The mice dig burrow systems, where they store food and spend the day. Young mice are born there in a nest chamber.

Wood mice use large hind feet to leap like kangaroos. They move fast, often bounding with front feet tucked up.

Wood mouse

Apodemus sylvaticus

95mm; longer tail

Widespread in all habitats – woodland to sand dunes, mountain-sides and gardens.

Seeds are the wood mouse's main food, along with shoots and buds. It also eats snails, nibbling through the shell, and a variety of insects and their larvae.

Large ears and eyes

White underparts

Yellow streak on chest

When mice are frightened, they often wash and groom themselves. They sit on their haunches and lick vigorously at their armpits, forelimbs and belly.

Autumn fruits such as hawthorn and other berries are part of the wood mouse's diet. It climbs well, and often uses places such as an old bird's nest high on a tree branch as a feeding place.

Its sandy-brown coat and large ears and eyes help to distinguish the wood mouse.

Long tail, lightly haired

Always cautious, the mice sniff suspiciously before approaching anything unfamiliar. They have an acute sense of smell and rely chiefly on odours as a means of recognising other mice.

A night-time woodland floor

MANY MAMMALS, large and small, live in deciduous woodland. The trees and shrubs provide more shelter than open country, and for climbing mammals there is extra living and foraging space among the branches. Above all, the many trees, shrubs and flowers offer a wide variety of food for the mammals. A wood covering about 65ha (160 acres) can support more than 5,000 mice and voles as well as many shrews, moles, squirrels and maybe some badgers and deer.

Predators such as tawny owls and weasels are attracted by the many small mammals. The night-flying tawny owl, especially, depends for food on the mice and voles that forage on the woodland floor, particularly in late autumn and winter when the vegetation dies back, making woodland mammals easier prey.

2 *The common dormouse ventures out only at night to forage among tree branches. In autumn it fattens up before hibernating about October in a nest built at or below ground level.*

1 *Wood mice feed on the nuts, fruits, seedlings and insects offered by the more open parts of the woodland floor. Several mice will share a space.*

3 Small woodland mammals are preyed on mainly by tawny owls. When mice and vole numbers are low, an owl may have trouble finding enough food to rear even one chick. Below its roost lie regurgitated pellets – wads of indigestible fur and bones from its prey.

5 Mice, voles and squirrels nibble the edge of caps of fungi, and leave fragments of the flesh lying about. At night slugs may feed on the cap, but make neat, rounded holes in it.

4 Bank voles forage among thick cover by day or night. They eat berries and seeds, nibble at fungi and take some insects.

YELLOW-NECKED MOUSE

NOT ONLY DOES the yellow-necked mouse look like a large, sandy-coloured wood mouse, but its behaviour is much the same. Both are nocturnal, with big ears and eyes to pick up faint sounds or slight movements that warn of danger, and both climb well and often search for food among high branches. Both are also found in woods, hedgerows and gardens. This seems to contradict a basic biological principle that no two animals can live in the same place and share the same food supply without one displacing the other. The yellow-necked mouse is larger, but it is the wood mouse that occurs over most of Britain. Yellow-necked mice occur only in the south, and even there huge tracts of suitable woodland seem to be without them. Where they do occur, yellow-necked mice may increase to high numbers and then inexplicably disappear a year or two later.

In parts of the south-east, where yellow-necked mice can be quite common, they often go into gardens and even houses in autumn – perhaps seeking a sheltered place for winter.

A nest of grass and leaves is made under-ground within the burrow. There are five or more babies in a litter. They emerge from the nest after about 18 days.

Good climbers, yellow-necked mice will search at the top of a tree for food such as new buds. They have been found as high up as 10m.

Yellow-necked mouse

Apodemus flavicollis

10cm; tail longer

Found in woods, hedgerows, but distribution is patchy. Much rarer than wood mouse.

Yellow
collar

Orange-
brown
flank

Like wood mice, yellow-necked mice
eat mainly seeds and fruit, such as
acorns, hazelnuts and blackberries.
In summer they also feed on insects
and small animals such as
snails and spiders.

The yellow-necked mouse
looks much like the wood
mouse, but is distinguished by
its distinct yellow collar. It is also
bigger and heavier than the wood
mouse, and its sandy-brown coat
has more orange on the flanks.

In autumn, yellow-necked mice often enter outbuildings or houses in search of food and shelter.
They are sometimes caught by cats or in traps.

WATER VOLE

OFTEN CALLED water rats, water voles are only distantly related to rats. Unlike brown rats, they prefer clean water in undisturbed areas by lowland river-banks or the fringes of ponds and lakes. Their numbers are declining rapidly in many areas, partly as a result of predation by an increasing population of mink, and they are now rare.

The water vole feeds almost entirely on waterside plants, and spends most of its life in a narrow strip of land at the water's edge. Small heaps of droppings mark the limits of its home range. A male occupies about 130m of bank, and often stays in the same area a long time, maybe all its life. A female occupies only half this range and will sometimes leave her regular haunts to live elsewhere. Young voles, which are dark brown with a long, almost black, tail, may be found away from water in damp woodland and grassy areas. Movement from a population often occurs when numbers are high after a good breeding season, or when shallow ponds dry up because of dry weather. A water vole lives around 12-18 months.

The voles live in a system of burrows in a waterside bank, with entrances above or below water. They swim by paddling with all four legs and are kept warm and dry by a short dense undercoat below long outer fur.

A nest of woven plant stems is sometimes made at the base of sedges on marshy ground. Usually the nest is below ground in a burrow system. Four or five litters of about five young can be reared between March and October.

Water vole
Arvicola terrestris
20cm; 12cm tail
Becoming rare in Britain and Ireland. Found by ponds and slow-running rivers.

Long, glossy, dark chocolate-brown fur

Although the water vole is about the same size as a brown rat, it differs in having a chubby face with a blunt nose, short furry ears and a shorter tail.

Chubby face

Completely black water voles occur, especially in Scotland. Voles with a white tail-tip are also more frequent in Scotland.

Active by day, the vole moves among grasses, sedges, willow shoots and other waterside plants. It grasps them in its forepaws to eat the best parts, leaving a trail of fragments and stumps.

BANK VOLE

AFTER THE WOOD MOUSE the bank vole is probably the most abundant of Britain's small rodents. It is more likely to be seen during daylight than the wood mouse, and tends to run and scurry rather than leap and bound. Although it is sometimes found in long grass, wet places or on mountains, the bank vole prefers to live around dense cover, rarely far from bramble thickets, hedgerows and other woody scrub. It is common also in country gardens. Few bank voles venture more than about 50m from the nest. Males generally range more widely than females.

In mild years when food is plentiful, bank voles may begin breeding early and continue well into late autumn. A vole born early in the year may itself be raising a family within a few weeks, so the population builds up quickly. But fewer than half of those born survive the first few months. After young voles leave the nest at about 18 days, they are often taken by predators such as weasels, or may die in cold, wet weather. The more robust survivors may live for 18 months.

There may be four or five litters, each with four or five babies, between April and September. The nest is sometimes above ground, perhaps in a tree crevice, but often up to 10cm below ground in a chamber reached by tunnels.

Where there is sufficient thick undergrowth, the bank vole forages busily by day or night along a network of tunnels beaten through vegetation or dug underground.

Bank vole

Clethrionomys glareolus

90mm; 60mm tail

Most common in lowlands. Found in woods, hedges and scrub. Very limited in Ireland.

Small ears
and eyes

Blunt nose

The bank vole can be distinguished from a
mouse by its chubby appearance, blunt nose,
small eyes and ears, and short, furry tail. Adults
have a glossy, chestnut-brown coat that
may shade to grey on the belly.

The bank vole has a redder
coat and more prominent ears
than a field vole. Young bank
voles are grey-brown and more
difficult to tell from field voles.

Short,
furry tail

Seeds, berries, nuts,
fruit, green plants
and fungi are all
part of the bank
vole's diet. Food
may be stored
underground or
taken there to
eat in safety.

Skomer vole
The Skomer vole
found on Skomer
Island, Pembrokeshire,
is twice as heavy as
mainland voles and
about 11.5cm long
in head and body. It
is one of four larger
island sub-species; the
others are on Jersey,
Mull and Raasay.

FIELD VOLE

OVERGROWN FIELDS and places with long, rough grass, particularly if damp and tussocky, are typically the home of the aptly named field vole. Aggressive and noisy, field voles utter loud squeaks and angry chattering as they defend their small territories, driving out other voles. Each vole makes runways among the grass stems, usually centred on the tussock where it nests; it feeds often, by day or night.

Field voles have a host of predators, but are prolific breeders. Numbers can multiply into the thousands – a vole plague – followed by a fast decline, as overcrowding and increased aggression affect breeding. These high and low populations occur at intervals of three to five years, accompanied often by similar fluctuations in predator levels. Field voles are abundant for a few years in young forestry plantations, but as the trees grow they cast a dense shade and the grass dies, forcing the voles to move on. Some survive on the fringes, from where they can recolonise grassy areas that develop once trees are felled. The normal lifespan is about a year.

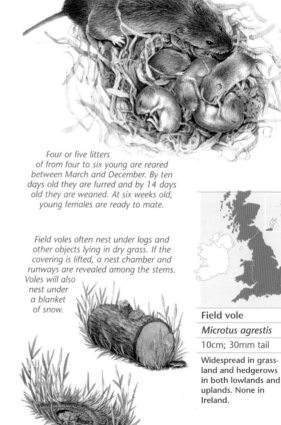

Four or five litters of from four to six young are reared between March and December. By ten days old they are furred and by 14 days old they are weaned. At six weeks old, young females are ready to mate.

Field voles often nest under logs and other objects lying in dry grass. If the covering is lifted, a nest chamber and runways are revealed among the stems. Voles will also nest under a blanket of snow.

Field vole

Microtus agrestis

10cm; 30mm tail

Widespread in grassland and hedgerows in both lowlands and uplands. None in Ireland.

Short ears

Blunt nose

Its yellowy-brown colouring helps to distinguish the field vole from the red-brown bank vole. It has a shorter, pinker tail and is also known as the short-tailed vole.

Yellowy-brown fur

Grass is the field vole's main food, particularly the succulent lower stems. It will also eat bulbs, roots and tree bark at ground level.

Short tail

Adults are belligerent. They compete for territory and are quick to fight in its defence.

Orkney vole
Microtus arvalis
Found only on the Orkney Islands in Scotland and the Channel Island of Guernsey, the deep brown Orkney vole is much like the field vole in habits and looks, but is heavier. It weighs 10-15g more.

COMMON DORMOUSE

IN PAST TIMES, the common dormouse was familiar to country folk. It was also named the hazel dormouse because it was often found in hazel coppices. Today common dormice are rarely seen, and no one is sure whether this is because they have become threatened, or are merely overlooked. When men spent many winter hours trimming hedges and cleaning out ditches, drowsy, hibernating dormice were often exposed. Many dormouse nests were also found when the poles were harvested from coppiced trees. Today these tasks, if done at all, are usually performed by machines, so dormice are much less likely to be noticed.

In summer dormice live in woodland shrubs and bushes or among tall hedges and dense scrub. They come out only at night to feed on insects, nuts and flowers. As they stay hidden among the branches they are not often caught by cats, nor do they normally venture into traps. Dormice may be taken by crows, magpies, owls and foxes, but can live to be about five years old in the wild.

Between May and September there is one litter, sometimes two, of from two to seven young, born blind and naked. They soon grow grey fur, but moult this before leaving the nest at a month old, when they resemble adults in colour but are greyer.

Pollen from catkins and spring flowers provides a dormouse with nutritious food. Its whiskers carry pollen from plant to plant, which aids pollination.

An agile climber, the dormouse will live in a bird's nest box, even one fixed high above the ground.

Common dormouse

Muscardinus avellanarius

75mm; 64mm tail

Uncommon. Found in southern hedges and woods. May occur in parts of northern England.

Secretive, nocturnal and rarely seen, the common dormouse is distinguished from all other mice by its fluffy tail, orange-yellow fur and chubby build. It also has smaller ears than other mice, but much bigger eyes than those of voles.

Orange-yellow fur

Creamy-white belly fur

Fluffy tail

A domed nest about 15cm across is built in a bush, often a thorny one to deter predators. The nest, built with dry leaves, moss, grass and strips of bark off shrubs, may be sited several feet above the ground.

Hazelnuts are often eaten. The dormouse makes a hole in the side of the shell to get at the kernel. The cut edge of the hole has toothmarks along it.

FAT DORMOUSE

THE ROMANS kept fat dormice in captivity and deliberately overfed them to make an unusual meal, so they are also known as edible dormice. In the wild these squirrel-like creatures eat extra food in late summer to build up reserves for winter.

The fat dormouse was not introduced to Britain until 1902, when a few were brought from the Continent and released at Tring in Hertfordshire. Now the dormice are found in many woodland and suburban areas of the Chilterns but have not spread much. The fat dormouse is not a wanderer and rarely travels more than a few hundred metres from its nest. It spends most time in tree branches, foraging only at night, so is rarely seen. But signs of the dormouse's activity are more evident; it chews the bark, buds and growing shoots of trees, and in autumn may enter a house or shed and gnaw woodwork or stored food. It also comes indoors to hibernate, and may scuttle about in a loft. It can make loud wheezing and churning noises.

A single litter of four or five young is produced each midsummer in a nest made of dry leaves and grass in a tree hollow or an old squirrel drey, or sometimes in the corner of a loft.

Sometimes the dormouse eats birds' eggs and nestlings, large insects and any small animals it can catch.

Fat dormouse

Glis glis

15cm; 12cm tail

Mainly confined to woodland in the Chilterns. It often winters in houses and sheds.

Fat dormice gnaw trees, particularly those with sweet, juicy sapwood under the bark. Fruit and timber trees may be severely damaged. Its tail helps the dormouse to balance.

Dark eye rings

The bushy-tailed fat dormouse looks like a small grey squirrel. Its fine grey body fur often has darker, brownish tinges on the tail, the outside of the legs and in a ring round each eye.

Grey body fur

White belly

Bushy grey-brown tail

From October to April the fat dormouse hibernates. It stays in the nest all the time and lives off its fat reserves, losing nearly half its weight.

Plant material is the main food, particularly fruits but also nuts, bark and fungi. The dormouse holds food in its forepaws while eating.

Grey squirrel

Fat dormouse

Although the fat dormouse may sit up like a squirrel, it keeps its tail laid flat. Fat dormice come out only at night, and grey squirrels are active only during the day.

RED SQUIRREL

RED SQUIRRELS are most likely to be seen in heavily forested areas soon after dawn. Mature Scots pine woods are a favourite habitat, but they are also found among other conifers such as larch and spruce. These trees provide a high thoroughfare among the branches and year-round food from seeds, buds, shoots and pollen, although the squirrels also like to forage for nuts among nearby deciduous trees.

The Scots pine was the only large native conifer to survive the last Ice Age, and the red squirrel one of the last mammals to colonise Britain before it was cut off from the rest of Europe 9,000 years ago. Until the 1940s the animal was fairly widespread. Now it has gone from much of Britain, its place taken by the grey squirrel. The reasons for the red squirrel's decline are unclear. One cause may be the loss of suitable woodland, and the felling of large areas of conifers. It is unlikely that grey squirrels drive away red, but they may stop them repopulating wooded areas by competing for food. Red squirrels live for about three years.

Most of the red squirrel's time is spent in the treetops, mostly among conifers, usually in extensive forests. On some trees squirrels strip bark to reach the sap. The squirrel uses strong, sharp claws to grip the bark as it runs head first down a tree, often scarring the bark. It is light enough to hang by just one foot.

The long, silky winter coat is chocolate brown, the fur on the back sometimes looking dark grey. The tail is a uniform dark brown. The red squirrel does not hibernate and is often seen in mid winter, though it cannot go more than a few days without eating.

Red squirrel

Sciurus vulgaris

20cm; 18cm tail

Declining; mostly gone from south. Mainly restricted to large areas of mature forest.

Ear tufts

Bushy
tail

Chestnut fur

The squirrel's ear tufts are
especially long in winter
(particularly on an adult), and
give it a perky appearance.

In summer the red squirrel has bright chestnut
fur with orange-brown feet and lower legs. Its
ear tufts may be smaller or absent in young
animals. As summer progresses, the squirrel's
bushy tail bleaches to a pale cream.

True albinos,
with pink eyes, are
sometimes seen in
Scotland. Very dark
brown varieties
also occur.

In autumn when food is plentiful, squirrels forage by
oak or beech trees for acorns, beechmast and other
foods to store for winter. They also eat heartily in
autumn to put on fat reserves for winter.

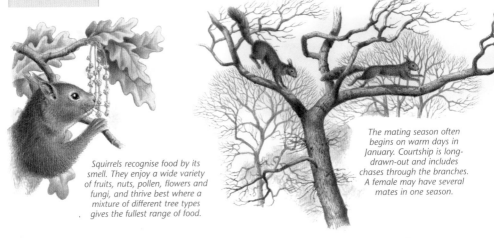

Squirrels recognise food by its smell. They enjoy a wide variety of fruits, nuts, pollen, flowers and fungi, and thrive best where a mixture of different tree types gives the fullest range of food.

The mating season often begins on warm days in January. Courtship is long-drawn-out and includes chases through the branches. A female may have several mates in one season.

Tree seeds and red squirrel survival

RED SQUIRREL NUMBERS from season to season depend on the seed crop of the dominant trees where they live. Where there are plenty of pine cones, hazelnuts or similar food, red squirrels build up generous fat reserves and many survive winter in good condition. Unlike the grey squirrel, though, they cannot digest acorns. They begin breeding early in the following year, and many babies are born and reared. In years with less abundant tree seeds, the squirrels begin winter with poor fat reserves and many die from starvation or disease, while most survivors are not fit enough to breed with any success. The

population can take years to recover, and where red squirrels are few, grey squirrels often move in. The struggling red squirrels are then forced to compete for food and space with a larger animal.

A litter of red squirrels usually numbers three or four, sometimes up to six, but in larger litters more die. Older females may produce two litters by the end of the breeding season in August. Males take no part in rearing young. A red squirrel is most in danger from predators for the first few months of life, after leaving the nest and before losing its fluffy, juvenile coat and becoming fully independent.

Young squirrels are born in a specially built drey with a thick, grassy lining inside a framework of twigs. It is about 30cm across and usually wedged against a tree trunk. Young are born blind and naked, but are fully furred by about three weeks old and open their eyes at four weeks.

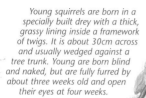

Food is held in the forepaws. Squirrels bite the scales off ripe pine cones to get at the seeds. Chewed cone cores and discarded scales litter the ground under the trees.

If the breeding nest is disturbed, a mother will carry her babies in her mouth one by one to an alternative nest nearby. Youngsters leave the nest at about two months old. Soon afterwards they become independent of their mother and develop an adult coat.

GREY SQUIRREL

ONE OF OUR most familiar mammals, the grey squirrel is a native of the hardwood forests of the eastern United States. It was introduced to Britain in the mid 19th century, but did not become established in the wild until about the turn of the 20th century.

Unlike native red squirrels, grey squirrels can live happily in hedgerow trees, parkland, gardens and other places without large areas of trees. Britain's patchwork countryside with dotted trees and isolated copses suited them well. Where grey squirrels spread to live alongside red squirrels, the greys became more numerous and displaced their smaller cousins, usually without obvious signs of conflict.

As well as nuts, acorns, beechmast and fungi, grey squirrels eat tree bark, leaves, shoots, buds and flowers. In commercial woodlands they damage trees and are a serious pest. But many find them attractive and endearing. Grey squirrels have few predators so can live for up to ten years. But most die younger, from starvation, accidents such as forest fires or from pest control.

A loud churring noise in the tree-tops often reveals the presence of grey squirrels as they aggressively scold or chase off an intruder.

Squirrels are active by day. They like to sit upright on vantage points to survey their surroundings, relying as much on eyesight as smell for information.

Grey squirrel

Sciurus carolinensis

25cm; 20cm tail

Common in forests, gardens, hedgerows: scarce on high ground. Range expanding.

Bushy,
grizzled tail

Winter fur, which begins
to grow in autumn, is
dense and a bright, silvery
grey with a brown tinge
along the middle of the
back. It is replaced by
brownish summer fur
during April and May.

No ear tufts

White
underparts

In summer the grey squirrel's
fur is often yellowish-brown, on the
flanks and feet especially. Its tail stays
the same colour all year.

Yellowish-brown fur

Silky black squirrels
are sometimes seen,
although rare. They
are found mainly in and
around Bedfordshire,
where black varieties
from North America
were released early in
the 20th century.

White squirrels
are fairly common,
in the south-east
especially. They
have pink eyes
and are true
albinos.

Usually a winter drey is on a sturdy branch close to the trunk.

Instead of building itself a drey, a grey squirrel may make its home in a hollow tree or a woodpecker's old nest hole.

A summer drey may be flimsy and lodged amid small branches.

The football-sized nest, or drey, is made of twigs, often with the leaves still attached. It is built fairly high in a tree and lined with dry grass and shredded bark.

The grey squirrel at home

BECAUSE GREY SQUIRRELS are agile, acrobatic and active by day, they are among the easiest and most interesting to watch of all British wild creatures. You might see them sitting surveying their surroundings, tails twitching to indicate uneasiness or suspicion, or hear them grinding their teeth aggressively and chattering loudly at an intruder or predator. You might also spot them scampering up and down trees, climbing walls or bounding along in short leaps.

Intelligent and resourceful, grey squirrels have been particularly successful at invading towns and gardens where there are trees. They become bold quickly, and soon learn to raid bird tables for extra food, or to chew through the string holding a nut basket suspended and collect their booty when it falls to the ground. Not only do they benefit from food put out for birds, they will also occasionally raid nests to steal eggs and nestlings. Young squirrels are born in tree-top dreys in spring or early summer. The average litter is three, and the male plays no part in the rearing. The youngsters disperse when their teeth are fully grown and they can feed themselves, usually at about ten weeks old. They breed for the first time at a year old.

The squirrel uses its forepaws to manipulate food, especially tough things such as nuts, which need a lot of gnawing to open. Nutshells litter the ground at a favourite feeding site.

Strong feet and sharp claws enable squirrels to climb brick walls to reach bird food on window sills.

Squirrels soon master the art of reaching a basket of nuts put out for birds.

Tree bark is gnawed to get at the nutritious sapwood below.

In late winter, courting squirrels often frisk and chase across lawns or along branches and logs.

Surplus food is stored for winter by burying. Often the cached food is not recovered, and acorns and other seeds sprout the following year, so aiding tree dispersal.

Alien rodents

PETS AND ZOO ANIMALS occasionally escape and may be seen in the wild. Even large animals such as zebras and sea lions sometimes get away, but are usually quickly recaptured. Small, agile rodents such as squirrels easily elude capture and may live wild for years. Occasionally small animals escape in a group and establish a breeding colony, as hamsters and gerbils have done many times, adding exotic species to Britain's wildlife.

Most alien animals do not survive long in the unsuitable conditions of a strange country, but some become well established and increase rapidly. They may then become pests that are hard to get rid of. Escaped coypus and musk rats have shown the damage that can be done by alien species that make a home in our countryside.

Indian giant squirrel
Ratufa indica
In the winter of 1959-60, an escaped giant squirrel lived wild in Blackheath, London, for several weeks before capture. No one knew how it got there. About 28cm head and body, tail same length.

Mongolian gerbil
Meriones unguiculatus
The hardy, soft-furred gerbil from the desert regions of Mongolia has been a popular pet in Britain since the 1960s. Many have escaped and established wild colonies, often under sheds and outbuildings. About 10cm head and body, tail same length.

Crested porcupine
Hystrix cristata
During the 1970s, a pair of crested porcupines escaped from a zoo in Staffordshire and lived free for about two years. At the same time there were some escaped Himalayan porcupines living free in Devon. All damaged trees, but did not seem to multiply. About 64cm head and body.

West Indian mouse
Nyctomys sumichastri
Dark-eyed, furry-tailed mice
have reached Britain from the
West Indies with cargoes of
bananas, which are part of their
diet. They normally arrive singly,
and have not established
colonies. About 12cm head
and body, tail same length.

Musk rat
Ondatra zibethicus
The semi-aquatic musk rat was brought to
Britain from North America in the 1920s for
fur farming. Some animals escaped to form
extensive colonies, and did a lot of damage
to crops. By 1937 the animal had been
exterminated. About 30cm head and
body, 25cm tail.

Coypu
Myocastor coypus
A native of South America, this large aquatic
rodent was introduced to Britain in 1929 for
its valuable fur. The animals soon escaped
and started breeding in the wild,
mainly in East Anglia where
they caused damage by eating
crops and burrowing into the
banks of drainage channels. They
were eventually eradicated in 1989.

Golden hamster
Mesocricetus auratus
A stoutly built burrower from eastern
Europe and the Middle East, the soft-
furred, nocturnal hamster feeds on
fruit, vegetables and grain. It stores
food in its large cheek pouches for
eating at leisure. About 18cm long,
including tail.

BROWN HARE

LARGE EYES and long ears provide the hare with sharp eyesight and hearing, warning of danger on the open downs or farmland it inhabits. The best time to see one is in the early morning or late evening as it sits up to survey the scene. Even when feeding it rarely keeps its head down for long. No other British mammal is better at surviving in an open habitat, where the cold, wind and rain are as much a challenge to survival as eluding predators.

Once brown hares were a common sight in pastures and ploughed fields, but numbers have declined markedly. Intensive farming may be a reason for the decline. When crops are harvested the land is often ploughed straight away, leaving a large area without food for hares. Weedkillers deprive them of vital food plants, while pesticide sprays may contaminate food and kill leverets. The young may also fall victim when crops are mown for silage.

A hare may live for three or four years. Predators such as foxes and owls take a few leverets, but adult hares are fast enough to elude most enemies.

Hares eat grass and other plants, but farm weedkillers destroy many of the plants they need. They also eat their own soft droppings.

If disturbed the hare can run as fast as 35 miles an hour – it runs with its tail held downwards, showing the dark topside. Normally it lopes along unhurriedly, its long hind legs placed in front of its forelegs at each stride.

Brown hare

Lepus europaeus

55cm; 10cm ears

Found in lowland grassland. Widespread but declining. Introduced into Ireland.

A leveret is born in the open with a full coat of fur and its eyes open. It lies low in a form – a depression made in the long grass. A litter usually numbers two or three, each kept in a separate form.

Black-tipped ears

Staring eyes

During the day the hare rests crouching low against the ground in scrub or grass or in a ploughed furrow. Its ears are laid flat and from a distance it looks like a large clod of earth or turf.

The brown hare is a shy, alert animal of open country. The male (Jack) is only slightly larger than the female (Jill).

Orange fur on throat and flanks

Powerful hind legs

MOUNTAIN HARE

HIGH HEATHER MOORS are the chief home of the mountain hare, and heather is its main food. The blue-grey tinge to its summer coat has also given it the name of blue hare. In summer its all-white tail helps to distinguish it from the rabbit and the brown hare, whose tails have dark tops. The mountain hare's dense white winter coat is more likely to turn wholly white in colder climates or at higher altitudes.

The hares feed mostly at night, resting during the day in a scraped hollow or a form nibbled out among the heather. On mountains they tend to move downhill to feed, returning to high ground to rest. In winter they move from the highest areas to shelter in hollows or hide among boulders. Mountain hares breed between February and August and may have three litters a year, each with four to six leverets. In some years more than three-quarters of hares die before the next breeding season. Some live to ten years.

In Ireland, mountain hares have replaced brown hares, living in all sorts of country including lowland pastures, and are often known as Irish hares.

In summer, the mountain hare supplements its heather diet with rushes, cotton grass and bilberry shoots. It regularly eats its own soft droppings.

In Ireland, mountain hares usually stay brown all year. They are often seen in large groups on farmland.

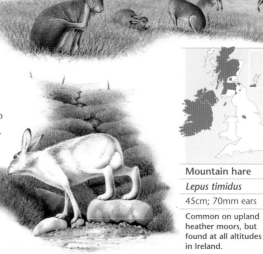

Regular pathways are made across the moors where mountain hares nibble their way through heather and bilberry scrub.

Mountain hare

Lepus timidus

45cm; 70mm ears

Common on upland heather moors, but found at all altitudes in Ireland.

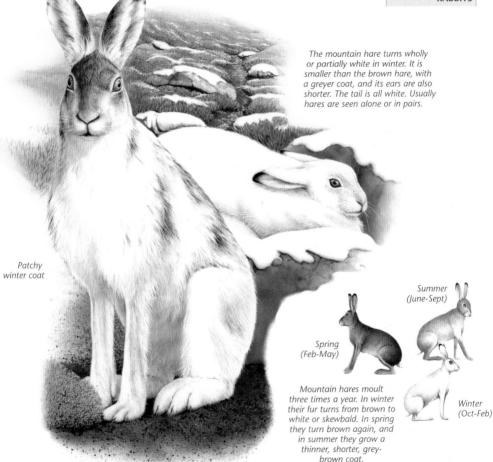

The mountain hare turns wholly or partially white in winter. It is smaller than the brown hare, with a greyer coat, and its ears are also shorter. The tail is all white. Usually hares are seen alone or in pairs.

Patchy winter coat

Spring (Feb-May)

Summer (June-Sept)

Winter (Oct-Feb)

Mountain hares moult three times a year. In winter their fur turns from brown to white or skewbald. In spring they turn brown again, and in summer they grow a thinner, shorter, grey-brown coat.

1 Red deer retreat from high ground for winter and live in the valleys. When spring comes they move back up the mountainsides to escape disturbance from people and pestilential flies.

2 Where there are meadow pipits there may also be pygmy shrews. Both feed on tiny insects among the stones and heather. Pygmy shrews keep well hidden but may be heard squeaking.

3 The stoat's white winter coat is good camouflage when hunting. It may also help to conserve body heat, because white fur radiates less energy than dark fur.

4 Many upland areas have commercial plantations of dense conifers. These rob mountain hares of living space but may provide a home for pine martens.

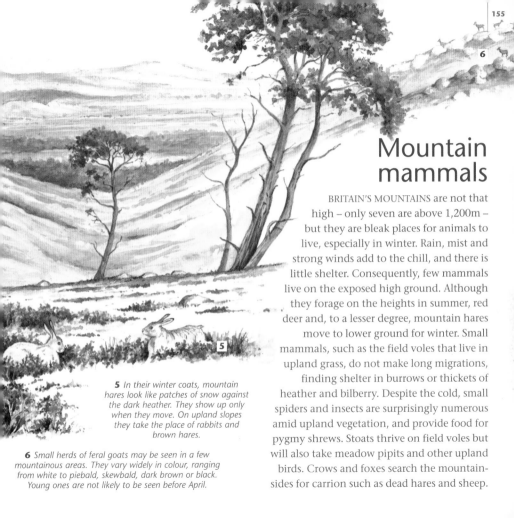

Mountain mammals

BRITAIN'S MOUNTAINS are not that high – only seven are above 1,200m – but they are bleak places for animals to live, especially in winter. Rain, mist and strong winds add to the chill, and there is little shelter. Consequently, few mammals live on the exposed high ground. Although they forage on the heights in summer, red deer and, to a lesser degree, mountain hares move to lower ground for winter. Small mammals, such as the field voles that live in upland grass, do not make long migrations, finding shelter in burrows or thickets of heather and bilberry. Despite the cold, small spiders and insects are surprisingly numerous amid upland vegetation, and provide food for pygmy shrews. Stoats thrive on field voles but will also take meadow pipits and other upland birds. Crows and foxes search the mountain-sides for carrion such as dead hares and sheep.

5 In their winter coats, mountain hares look like patches of snow against the dark heather. They show up only when they move. On upland slopes they take the place of rabbits and brown hares.

6 Small herds of feral goats may be seen in a few mountainous areas. They vary widely in colour, ranging from white to piebald, skewbald, dark brown or black. Young ones are not likely to be seen before April.

RABBIT

IT WAS NOT UNTIL the 12th century that Britain saw rabbits. They were introduced from the Continent as a valuable source of meat and skins. For long they were a profitable part of the rural economy, but in the past 200 years have become major pests.

Rabbits are sociable and live in colonies in burrow systems known as warrens, where a status system rules. Dominant rabbits – male or female – claim and mark a territory in the best part of the warren and are more successful at breeding than subordinate rabbits. Subordinate do not establish a territory, and mix amicably together. But if one enters the territory of a dominant individual, it is driven off.

Most rabbit activity takes place at night and close to the warren. The animals rarely move more than 140m from home, so the vegetation near the warren is kept short by frequent grazing. This leaves a wide, open area for revealing the approach of predators – rabbits have a keen sense of smell and hearing and their prominent eyes are set so they can see all ways at once.

When danger threatens, a rabbit warns others in the colony by thumping with the hind foot. A flash of white from the underside of the tail (scut) as it runs away also serves as an alarm signal.

Shallow scrapes in the turf, exposing patches of soil, are common around warrens. They are made as territory markers. A rabbit may be seen 'chinning' – rubbing the ground with its chin, which has scent-secreting glands. This is done to mark the rabbit's territory.

Rabbit

Oryctolagus cuniculus

45cm

Common. Increasing in many areas. Found mainly in farmland and lowland forests.

Rabbits are smaller than hares and have shorter ears without big black tips. The female (doe) is smaller than the male (buck) and has a narrower head.

Greyish-brown fur

Orange nape

Short tail, black on top, white underneath

Rabbits keep their fur clean by regular washing and grooming, using tongue, teeth and claws.

Ant hills make good lookout points. Many have rabbit droppings on top, being used as rabbit latrines and to mark the limit of a territory.

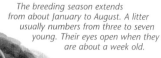

The breeding season extends from about January to August. A litter usually numbers from three to seven young. Their eyes open when they are about a week old.

The breeding nest is in a dead-end burrow, or stop, often separate from the main warren. The doe lines it with fur plucked from her chest.

Rabbit families

IN ONE YEAR a female rabbit can have more than 20 offspring, many of which will themselves breed when only four months old. Such prolific breeding is countered by deaths from cold, wet, disease and predators. Well over three-quarters of all rabbits live less than one year. The introduction of the flea-borne virus disease myxomatosis, in 1954, caused the deaths of more than 95 per cent of Britain's rabbits, and also brought about a decline in the numbers of buzzards, foxes, stoats and other predators that fed mainly on rabbits. Now rabbits are once more common, having developed a resistance to the virus, and are again damaging crops.

Rabbit warrens used to be sited in open fields but, because of frequent cultivation and deep ploughing, are now more often in hedgerows or at field edges. From here the rabbits venture out to nibble plants and gnaw tree bark, mostly in the dark. While underground during the day, a rabbit eats the soft droppings of food that it has already digested once to absorb nutrients still in the droppings. The hard, dark, second droppings are deposited above ground.

Young rabbits leave the nest at about three weeks, and are weaned about a week after that.

Green plants of many kinds are eaten, nibbled off close to the ground as the rabbit works round in a semi-circle. Rabbits do occasionally drink, but usually get sufficient moisture from their intake of green food.

Trees are damaged by rabbits eating bark and will die if the bark is eaten all round the trunk. Plantations often have rabbit-proof fences, or young trees are fitted with protective 'collars'.

Rabbits and the landscape

WITHOUT RABBITS, much more downland and clifftop would be bramble and hawthorn scrub rather than short turf studded with flowers. Rabbits suppress shrubs by nibbling new shoots but tend not to eat older shrubs, leaving established thickets. These provide rabbits with shelter from buzzards, but give cover to hunting foxes. Nibbling rabbits are damaging to crops, so farmers try to fence off their fields. But rabbits are tolerated on coastal strips unsuitable for crops because of exposure to wind and salt spray.

By their close and constant grazing, rabbits crop grass short, encouraging low-growing or creeping plants such as vetches and trefoils. These attract butterflies such as the common blue, which feed on nectar and lay their eggs on the plants, which are eaten by the caterpillars. The short turf is also ideal for other insects, especially ants. The insects in turn attract many species of birds such as skylarks.

1 For buzzards, rabbits are a major food. As with foxes and stoats, their chances of survival and successful breeding increase with an abundance of rabbits.

2 Rabbits feed mostly at night, but in undisturbed places will graze by day. Turf near a burrow may be cropped very short, but thistles are avoided.

2

4 Nettles and elder bushes thrive near a warren, where the soil has been enriched with nitrogen from rabbit droppings.

5 Rabbit-proof fencing extends 30cm underground. It protects sprouting corn, carrots, turnips and other crops from nibbling rabbits.

3 The warren (burrow system) is dug in deep soil and has many entrances. Birds such as puffins and jackdaws may take over old clifftop burrows.

6 Short turf favours orchid growth. It also encourages insects because it warms quickly in the sun, faster than ground under long grass.

MOLE

A MOLE IS A RARE sight, spending much of its life in a burrow system that it tunnels underground. The soil heaps (molehills) it makes while tunnelling give away its presence. Active all year, moles are found in most places except ground above 1,000m and in very acid soils. In woodlands, where they are quite common, molehills are often hidden by leaves.

Moles come to the surface to collect nesting material – dry grass and leaves – and also to look for food when the soil is dry. Their main food is earthworms, which, being full of soil, are heavy but not very nutritious, so moles eat at least half their body weight in food every day. Moles are most vulnerable to predators when above ground, even though they emerge mainly at night. Their skin glands make them distasteful to carnivorous mammals, but large numbers are eaten by tawny owls and barn owls. About a third of moles survive for more than a year, but few live to be three years old.

The mole can run backwards through its tunnels. Sensitive hairs on its tail detect any obstacles, and its velvety fur will lie backwards or forwards so that it does not jam against the tunnel walls.

Colour variation is more frequent than among other animals, perhaps because the variant moles, living underground, are less likely to attract the attention of predators. Apricot, creamy-white, pale grey and piebald moles may be found.

The mole is not blind, but each eye is only about the size of a pinhead. It finds its way in the darkness underground by means of sensitive whiskers and touch sensors on its nose.

Mole

Talpa europaea

15cm

Found in all types of country except high moors, mountains. Lives mostly underground.

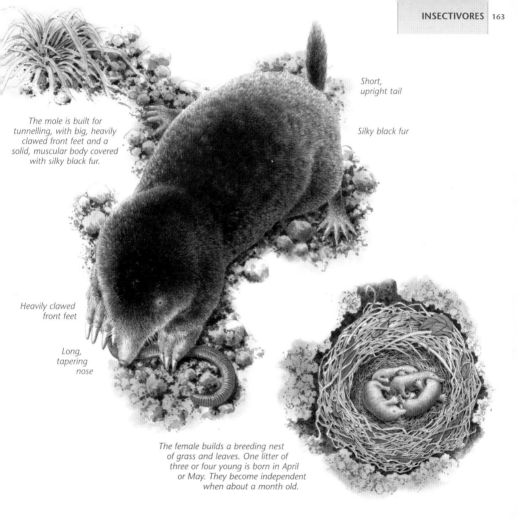

Short, upright tail

Silky black fur

The mole is built for tunnelling, with big, heavily clawed front feet and a solid, muscular body covered with silky black fur.

Heavily clawed front feet

Long, tapering nose

The female builds a breeding nest of grass and leaves. One litter of three or four young is born in April or May. They become independent when about a month old.

A mole's life underground

IN THE EYES of many gardeners and farmers, moles are a nuisance. They dig tunnels close to ground level, which may interfere with the roots of garden plants and crops. Occasionally tunnels are so near the surface that the soil is forced up in a long ridge – once thought (wrongly) to be 'love runs' made by male moles seeking a mate. Molehills each contain about 1kg of soil. They disfigure lawns and in fields can hinder or damage farm machinery such as combine harvesters. But moles can also be useful. They eat a lot of insect larvae that damage grass and root crops, and their tunnelling helps to aerate the soil – important in peaty and waterlogged areas.

In days gone by, country parishes often employed a mole catcher to trap and dig up moles where they were not wanted. In turn he sold the skins for hat and coat trimmings. As late as the 1950s about a million moles were trapped every year in Britain. Synthetic furs saved moles from this fate.

Each mole has its own burrow, a system of firm-walled tunnels about 5cm wide and 4cm high which may be about 200m long.

When tunnelling, a mole uses one front foot to force soil upwards into a molehill while it braces the other, and its hind feet, against the walls of the tunnel. It can move twice its own weight of soil – more than 200g – a minute

As well as travelling backwards in its tunnel, a mole can also turn in the opposite direction by doing a forward roll.

Molehills are heaps of displaced soil pushed to the surface up vertical tunnels at intervals while a mole is burrowing. They are not burrow entrances. Molehill soil is loose and fresh, unlike an ant hill, which is steep-sided and grassy.

Fortress

A mole does spend some of its time on the surface, especially at night. This is when it is most likely to be caught by a predator such as an owl.

Long soil ridge

The breeding nest is the size of a football. It usually has several exits. An extra large molehill, or fortress, may cover the nest chamber in early spring.

The mole is aggressive and normally chases an intruding mole from its burrow, except briefly for mating in late February or March.

A mole regularly patrols its tunnels to eat whatever soil animals – such as worms, beetle larvae and slugs – have fallen from the walls. Tunnels are longest and molehills most numerous in poor soil, where the mole's food supply is sparse.

Highways and havens

1 *Voles, mice and beetles on mown verges are prey for hovering kestrels.*

2 *Rabbits dig their warrens in well-drained, undisturbed embankments. They usually feed in nearby fields, not on oily, gritty, roadside vegetation.*

THE GRASSLAND and scrub along the broad verges of major roads and motorways offer a comparatively safe home to animals that can tolerate traffic noise. Moles, particularly, benefit as no one ploughs up their burrows, and because traffic vibration brings worms, their major food, to the surface. Small mammals such as voles and shrews abound, and foxes and rabbits are quite common. The varied plant life offers food and cover to some small mammals, but it is often contaminated with salt and oil from the road surface and car fumes.

Road verges act as corridors along which animals spread into cities and across wide areas of country. But crossing roads is a problem. Some mammals manage it – even slow-moving moles – but rabbits, hedgehogs, deer and other night-time animals are often dazzled by headlights and get run over. Thousands a year die on the roads; their bodies help to feed scavengers such as foxes, crows and magpies.

3 *Early in the morning crows feed on the night's road casualties, such as hares, hedgehogs and rabbits.*

4 Moles living on motorway verges are safe from farm ploughs. Molehills are often numerous on the central reservation, and as they do not contain road rubble, the moles must have crossed the road above ground, not by tunnelling.

HEDGEHOG

BRITAIN'S ONLY SPINY mammal, the hedgehog has been a familiar creature of gardens, hedgerows and meadows for centuries. Folk stories tell of hedgehogs picking up fruit on their spines and sucking milk from cows, but such behaviour is improbable.

Beetles, caterpillars and earthworms make up most of the hedgehog's diet, but it will also eat birds' eggs, slugs, snails and carrion. In winter, when small animals are in short supply, the hedgehog hibernates in a nest of leaves and grass and lives off body fat built up in autumn. Hedgehogs are ready to breed in April, soon after hibernation ends. Most young are born in early summer, though there are some late litters in September. Late-born young often do not survive winter. A mother disturbed in her nest may eat or abandon new-born young, but will carry older ones by the scruff of the neck to a safer place. Youngsters start to take solid food at about a month, and at night the mother leads her family out to forage. The young become independent at about six weeks.

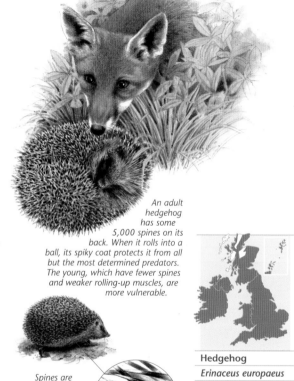

An adult hedgehog has some 5,000 spines on its back. When it rolls into a ball, its spiky coat protects it from all but the most determined predators. The young, which have fewer spines and weaker rolling-up muscles, are more vulnerable.

Spines are modified hairs that can be raised for defence. They are about 25mm long and sharp. Each spine lasts for a year or more before it drops out and a replacement is grown.

Hedgehog

Erinaceus europaeus

25cm

Widespread on farmland and in urban areas. Scarce on moors, and in conifer forests.

Spiny coat

Long, coarse hair on face and underparts

From three to five young are born, usually in June or July, in a nest of leaves and grass. The young are blind and pink at first, but sprout a few white, bristly spines within hours of birth.

During the first two weeks of life, young hedgehogs grow more and more brown spines alongside the white spines. Their eyes open at about 14 days old. By the time they are five to six weeks old, they have more than 2,000 spines.

A hedgehog is active mostly at night, but young or sickly animals may be seen by day. It relies mainly on smell to find food.

Although hedgehogs can swim well, they often drown in swimming pools and even tiny garden ponds because they cannot climb the smooth sides. A strip of wire netting fixed to the side aids escape.

Cattle grids, trenches and similar holes are a danger to hedgehogs because they often fall in and cannot get out. Their spines may act as a cushion and make them less afraid of falling than most animals. Many cattle grids now have ramps or tunnels which allow hedgehogs to escape.

Helping hedgehogs to survive

ALTHOUGH FEW ANIMALS prey on them, hedgehogs face many hazards. Thousands are killed every year by motor vehicles because they roll up in the face of danger. Though hedgehogs can run quite fast, the theory that more are tending to run from danger has little evidence to support it. As hedgehogs feed on garden pests, it is in a gardener's interest to encourage them. But there are dangers for hedgehogs in gardens, too, if they get stuck in ponds or tangled up in netting. Garden chemicals such as insecticides and slug pellets also pose a threat to hedgehog survival. Many such chemicals are present in minute quantities in beetles and caterpillars, and as hedgehogs eat hundreds of them every month they can soon accumulate enough poison to damage their health.

Hedgehogs face their greatest risks during hibernation. They may die of cold or be disturbed by fire or flood, or someone may wreck their nest. Gardeners can help by leaving piles of fallen leaves undisturbed behind sheds and under hedges. More than half of all hedgehogs do not survive their first winter. The remainder may live two or three years, rarely five or six.

Extra food such as cat or dog food helps garden hedgehogs to fatten up for winter hibernation. They will travel more than 400m for such a treat. A hedgehog will die during winter if its reserves of body fat are inadequate.

If a hedgehog is seen to froth at the mouth and twist itself about, it is not sick but is spreading the frothy saliva on its fur and spines with its tongue. The purpose of this behaviour is unknown, but it is quite normal.

Hedgehogs sniff through garden litter to nose out woodlice and slugs. Eating poisoned creatures can lead to a hedgehog's death, so avoid using garden chemicals.

1 *The carrion crow finds the hedgerow a good place to scavenge for dead rabbits or voles. Hawthorn berries provide sustenance for noisy flocks of fieldfares.*

A winter hedgerow

2 *Rabbits scrape away the snow with their forepaws to search for grass and other plants to eat. Hedgerows often shelter rabbit warrens.*

ON COLD winter days the countryside is still and silent, with only a few birds or the odd rabbit about. In winter weather it is hard for animals to keep warm, and frost and snow make it difficult to find food. Digging for worms is impossible in frozen ground, and it is too cold for many small creatures such as beetles to be found.

Hedgehogs and dormice avoid the problem by hibernating in a weatherproof nest, often at the bottom of a hedge. Instead of trying to find enough food to provide sufficient energy to keep warm, they allow their bodies to cool down and remain inactive for weeks on end until better weather returns. For some animals, snow is a welcome protection. On a clear, frosty night, a brown hare crouched on the surface may have to endure an air temperature of –8°C. But a mouse under the snow is protected from the cold air and exposed only to snow temperature – about 0°C. Inside its hedgerow nest or burrow it can even generate enough heat to be quite warm – perhaps at a temperature of 20°C or more.

4 A grey squirrel's winter drey in a hedgerow oak is easy to see when the tree is bare. The squirrel does not hibernate and is often out in the snow searching for buried acorns.

5 A magpie's domed nest is similar to a grey squirrel's drey, but it does not have any leaves clinging to the outside.

6 Dead leaves make the most weatherproof winter nest for a hibernating hedgehog. The hedgehog carries the leaves to its chosen site and piles them in a heap supported by brambles or brushwood. It burrows into the heap and shuffles round until the leaves are all firmly packed into the walls of the nest.

7 Inside its winter nest, a harvest mouse is warm and snug under the snow layer. It does not hibernate, but forsakes the upper areas of tall grass and shrubs to live on the ground.

3 Unlike the hedgehog, the field vole is active throughout winter. It tunnels among the grass underneath the snow, eating blades and stems.

8 Old summer nest of a harvest mouse

COMMON SHREW

NO COMMON SHREW can tolerate another in its territory, except briefly at breeding time. When two common shrews meet, both scream with shrill, aggressive squeaks, which may be the origin of 'shrewish' as a term for a scolding woman. The squeaks, heard for some distance, are often the only sign that shrews are nearby. They spend much of their time underground so are rarely seen, but are probably one of Britain's most abundant mammals.

Active by day or night, the shrew is constantly on the move, twittering and muttering and poking its long nose here and there as it scurries along in search of food such as woodlice. It snatches a brief rest every hour or two, but expends so much energy that it will starve if it goes without food for more than a few hours. The shrew forages in the soil or leaf litter, along tiny tunnels it digs itself or which have been made by small rodents.

Common shrews may live to be 18 months. Many fall prey to owls, other predators being deterred by the foul-tasting glands in the shrew's skin.

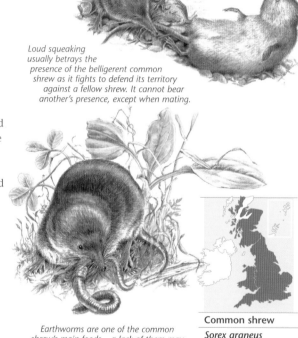

Loud squeaking usually betrays the presence of the belligerent common shrew as it fights to defend its territory against a fellow shrew. It cannot bear another's presence, except when mating.

Earthworms are one of the common shrew's main foods – a lack of them may limit its numbers in places such as moorland. It also eats other soil animals and many insects, consuming almost its own weight in food daily.

Common shrew

Sorex araneus

76mm; 40mm tail

Common in hedgerows, fields and woods, but scarce on moorland. None in Ireland.

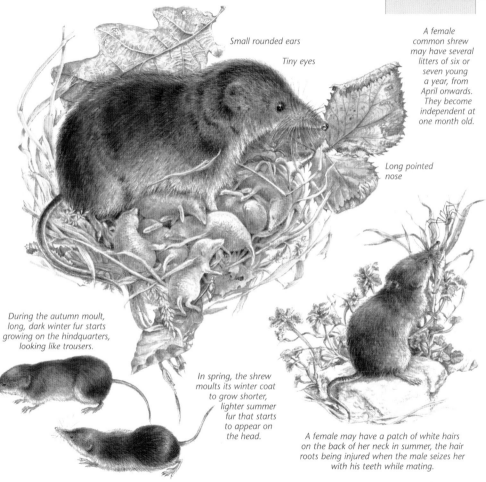

Small rounded ears

Tiny eyes

A female common shrew may have several litters of six or seven young a year, from April onwards. They become independent at one month old.

Long pointed nose

During the autumn moult, long, dark winter fur starts growing on the hindquarters, looking like trousers.

In spring, the shrew moults its winter coat to grow shorter, lighter summer fur that starts to appear on the head.

A female may have a patch of white hairs on the back of her neck in summer, the hair roots being injured when the male seizes her with his teeth while mating.

PYGMY SHREW

THE PYGMY SHREW is Britain's smallest mammal, not much bigger than a stag beetle. It is so tiny that it is near the limit at which a warm-blooded animal can exist – if it were any smaller its body surface would be too extensive for its bulk and it would lose heat too rapidly to maintain a warm body temperature. The shrew loses so much energy as body heat that it must constantly search for food, and will starve if it fails to eat for more than 2 hours. Hardly ever pausing for more than a few minutes in its busy foraging, the pygmy shrew may explore more than 1,250m² of territory regularly. It bustles along shallow tunnels made in the soil, leaf litter or vegetation, and avidly eats small soil creatures such as spiders, tiny beetles and insect larvae.

Females give birth to several litters each summer. The young grow quickly and leave the nest at about three weeks old. But many shrews die within a few months of birth, and those that survive to breed the following year do not live through a second winter.

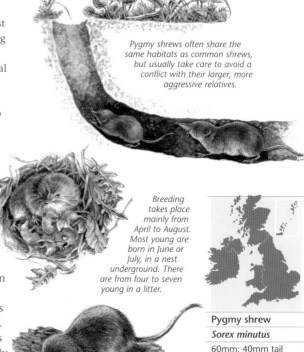

Pygmy shrews often share the same habitats as common shrews, but usually take care to avoid a conflict with their larger, more aggressive relatives.

Breeding takes place mainly from April to August. Most young are born in June or July, in a nest underground. There are from four to seven young in a litter.

Pygmy shrew

Sorex minutus

60mm; 40mm tail

Found on farmland, moors and in forests. Widespread, but scarcer than common shrew.

Compared with other shrews, the pygmy shrew has a bulbous head and a short, narrow snout.

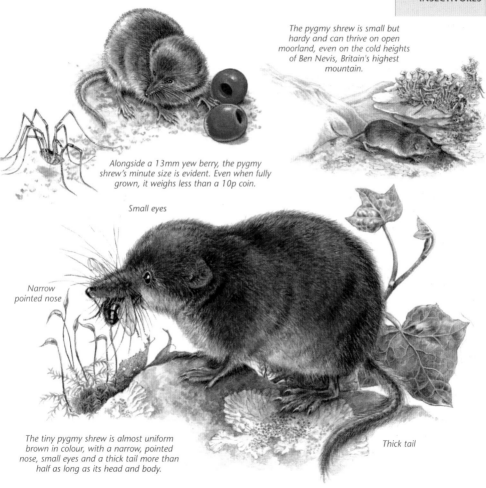

The pygmy shrew is small but hardy and can thrive on open moorland, even on the cold heights of Ben Nevis, Britain's highest mountain.

Alongside a 13mm yew berry, the pygmy shrew's minute size is evident. Even when fully grown, it weighs less than a 10p coin.

Small eyes

Narrow pointed nose

The tiny pygmy shrew is almost uniform brown in colour, with a narrow, pointed nose, small eyes and a thick tail more than half as long as its head and body.

Thick tail

WATER SHREW

ALL SHREWS TEND to be more abundant in damp places, where their prey, such as worms, insect larvae and small spiders, is common. Water shrews will also take to the water to hunt in ponds and streams for fish, tadpoles and even frogs. They can also live away from the water, even on dry downland, and some inhabit stony beaches where they probably feed on sand hoppers and flies along the high-tide line. Active by day or night, the shrews eat roughly their own weight in food daily.

Except for females raising families, water shrews normally live alone in shallow burrows they dig themselves. Sometimes a burrow is in a bank and has an underwater entrance. Two or three litters of three to eight young may be born in a year, from May onwards. Some females have their first litter when only two or three months old, but most do not breed until the summer following their birth. Although they may live for up to 18 months, water shrews mostly die young or are taken by predators such as owls, pike and mink.

Prey is usually caught from behind and, if taken in the water, hauled ashore to be eaten. Mild poison in its saliva may help the water shrew to subdue large prey such as a frog.

Bristly hairs along the underside of the tail and a hairy fringe on each hind toe are aids to paddling and steering while swimming.

Water shrew

Neomys fodiens

86mm; 55mm tail

Found in farmland, woods and hedgerows. Widespread, but may be scarce in some areas.

The water shrew's black coat and silvery-white underparts meet in a sharp line along its flanks. Juveniles have duller coats than adults.

Black coat

White eyebrows and ear tips

All-black animals are found more often than among other types of shrew. Other colour variants are rare.

Young water shrews leave the nest at about four weeks old. Families often travel in procession – the mother leads and the others hold the one in front.

LESSER WHITE-TOOTHED SHREW

UNLIKE ANY OTHER British shrews, which all have red-tipped teeth, white-toothed shrews have all-white teeth. There are two species, lesser and greater, neither found on the mainland. The lesser white-toothed shrew is found on the Isles of Scilly, and on Jersey and Sark in the Channel Islands. It may have come to the islands in boatloads of animal fodder from southern or eastern Europe. The greater white-toothed shrew lives in the Channel Islands.

Normally the Scilly shrew lives under logs or dense vegetation or among stones, out of sight of predators such as kestrels. It keeps within about 50m of its nest. The mild climate of the islands permits a long breeding season, from early summer until late autumn. The young take about three weeks to reach weaning age, by when their mother is often pregnant again. A female sometimes leads her family out in a long procession each one grasping the animal in front. Most white-toothed shrews die early, but some can live for well over a year.

The young are born in a nest of grass and leaves often sited among boulders or under tree roots. There may be three or four litters of up to six young in one season.

Greater white-toothed shrew
Crocidura russula

Sometimes called the musk shrew because of its strong scent, the greater white-toothed shrew lives in farmland and hedgerows on the Channel Islands of Alderney, Guernsey and Herm. It is particularly common around buildings in dry places. It differs from the lesser species only in its tooth pattern.

Insects and other small creatures such as snails are all part of the shrew's diet. It eats nearly its own weight in food every day.

Projecting tail hairs

Big ears

Greater White-toothed Shrew
Lesser White-toothed Shrew

Lesser white-toothed shrew

Crocidura suaveolens

60mm; 40mm tail

In Britain found only in the Isles of Scilly and the Channel Islands. Except on Jersey, white-toothed shrews are the only shrews present. The lesser and greater species never occur together on the same island.

The lesser white-toothed shrew, or Scilly shrew, is often found on the shores of the Isles of Scilly, where it forages for sand hoppers among damp seaweed and boulders.

The shrew has big scent glands in the skin of the flanks and by the tail. They give off a musky scent. The flank glands are sometimes exposed when the animal is running about.

HOW ALL BATS ARE BUILT

A bat has a mouse-like, furry body and large wings. Each wing is a modified hand, with a small, hooked thumb and four other long digits which support the membranes. The wing membranes stretch to meet the hind legs on each side. The hind legs bend backwards at the knee and are outer supports for the tail membrane; a short heel spur (calcar) supports it at each ankle. The tail runs down the middle of the membrane.

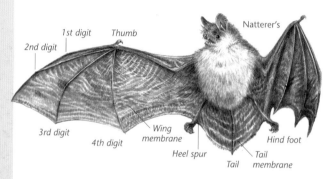

1st digit
Thumb
2nd digit
Natterer's
3rd digit
4th digit
Wing membrane
Heel spur
Hind foot
Tail
Tail membrane

FACIAL DIFFERENCES

No fleshy spike in ear

Greater horseshoe

Nose-leaf

Horseshoe bat *The bat has a horseshoe-shaped fold of skin round the nostrils, with a triangular lobe projecting up between the eyes. The ears lack a tragus – a fleshy central spike or lobe.*

Dog-like muzzle

Fleshy spike in ear

Serotine

Ordinary bat *The bat has a dog-like muzzle with no nose-leaf. But it has a tragus – a fleshy spike (or central lobe) – in each ear. The shape of the tragus varies with each species of bat.*

Horseshoe & ordinary bats

THERE ARE CLOSE to 1,000 species of bats across the world, in 19 families. Britain has only two of the families, the *Rhinolophidae*, or horseshoe bats, and the *Vespertilionidae*, or ordinary bats. There are two British species of horseshoe bats and about a dozen of ordinary bats.

Bats are the only mammals capable of flying long distances, using a modified form of the limbs common to all mammals. Scientists classify bats as the Order *Chiroptera*, which means hand-wing. Bats do not walk far and have poorly developed hind limbs.

When flying fast and in the dark, bats avoid obstacles and track down prey by means of elaborate echolocation systems similar to the radar used in ships and aircraft. Horseshoe bats emit sound through the nostrils, focused into a narrow beam by a fleshy, cone-shaped trumpet

WINGS AND TAILS COMPARED

Greater horseshoe

Pipistrelle

Horseshoe bat
The wings are broad and rounded. They allow slow, unhurried, rather than fluttery flight, and easy turning in small spaces such as caves. The tail is short and the membrane shallow.

Ordinary bat
The wings are narrower and more pointed at the tips. Some species, such as the noctule, have particularly long, narrow wings that allow fast flight but less ability to manoeuvre in small spaces. The tail is usually longer than that of a horseshoe bat, with a deeper membrane, but the pattern varies according to the species.

Greater horseshoe

Noctule

DIFFERENT WAYS OF RESTING

Horseshoe bat *The bat rests by hanging upside down and gripping with its toes. It sleeps with wings wrapped round it like a shawl. Its rounded body makes crawling difficult, so the bat needs a roost to which it can fly direct.*

Ordinary bat *The bat roosts by hanging, head down, with wings folded. It can squeeze into crevices in bricks or wood. It has a flat body and can crawl with wings folded, using its forelimbs as legs and its hooked thumbs to grip the surface.*

on the snout. The bat moves its head from side to side to scan ahead. Ordinary bats emit sound through the mouth, and have in each ear a fleshy spike known as a tragus, which is part of their sound-reception system.

All British bats eat insects, and as these are scarce in winter the bats hibernate during the coldest months. Many bats make seasonal migrations to hibernating places.

LESSER HORSESHOE BAT

THE LESSER HORSESHOE bat is a delicate, much smaller edition of the greater horseshoe bat, and more often solitary. Like its larger cousin, the bat likes to hibernate in damp cellars, mines or tunnels in winter, so lives only where such places are available. Its choice of roosts is wider, for it can fly in a tunnel only 15cm high, or up a shaft only 50cm wide. In Britain lesser horseshoe bats do not travel far from their regular haunts, but on the Continent journeys of up to 150km have been recorded.

The bats mate in autumn and winter, but the embryo does not begin to develop until April. A female gives birth to only one baby a year, usually in July or August in an attic, a hollow tree or an old building. Youngsters can fly around the roost at three weeks, and all can look after themselves by late August. Young bats do not normally breed until their second year. Although a lesser horseshoe bat is similar in size to a common shrew, its lifespan is probably four or five times longer, possibly because it hibernates.

A horseshoe bat's nose-leaf is used to direct the high-pitched sounds it emits to navigate or find its prey, locating it by the echoes. The lesser horseshoe has the highest-frequency sound pulses of any British bat, which help it to locate tiny prey.

Horseshoe bats need roosts where they can hang freely. They do not hide in crevices like other kinds of bat. Lesser horseshoe bats often use cellar ceilings, or may hang from a protruding nail.

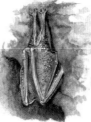

A hibernating horseshoe bat wraps its wings round its body. As it hibernates in a humid place, it is often covered with tiny droplets of condensation.

Lesser horseshoe bat

Rhinolophus hipposideros

40mm body; 25cm wingspan

Found where there are caves or mines for hibernation. A few recorded from east England.

The lesser horseshoe bat has a body smaller than a man's thumb, and is one of Britain's tiniest mammals. Like the greater horseshoe bat, it has a nose-leaf (horseshoe-shaped skin round the nostrils), a rounded body and broad wings.

Its broad, rounded wings enable a horseshoe bat to fly slowly, hover or fly in a narrow space such as a chimney. Lesser horseshoe bats eat tiny insects such as gnats, caught in their jaws in flight.

GREATER HORSESHOE BAT

ONCE COMMON IN southern Britain, greater horseshoe bats are now in danger of extinction. Like other bats, they have suffered from the decline in the number of places where insects abound – such as hedges and ponds – as well as from eating insects contaminated with pesticides. Also, they like a warm climate and southern Britain is the extreme northern limit of their range. If there are several cold or wet summers, the bats do not breed very successfully and the young struggle to survive their first year.

Greater horseshoe bats also need space for winter hibernation – large, humid places such as old mines, caves or tunnels that may be frequently disturbed or blocked up for safety. Efforts have been made to protect the bats' breeding and hibernation sites and, like other British bats, they are protected by law. But this may not be enough to save a species whose numbers have shrunk to less than a tenth of what they were 50 years ago.

Large prey such as a cockchafer beetle may be taken from near the ground, the bat swooping low to grab the creature in its jaws.

The bat cannot crawl. It flies straight to a roost and hangs by gripping the rough surface with its claws. A bat's weight keeps its toes gripped; it bends its knees to release itself.

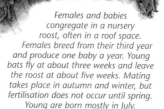

Females and babies congregate in a nursery roost, often in a roof space. Females breed from their third year and produce one baby a year. Young bats fly at about three weeks and leave the roost at about five weeks. Mating takes place in autumn and winter, but fertilisation does not occur until spring. Young are born mostly in July.

Greater horseshoe bat

Rhinolophus ferrumequinum

65mm body; 35cm wingspan

Declining. Found only where suitable hibernation places and conditions still exist.

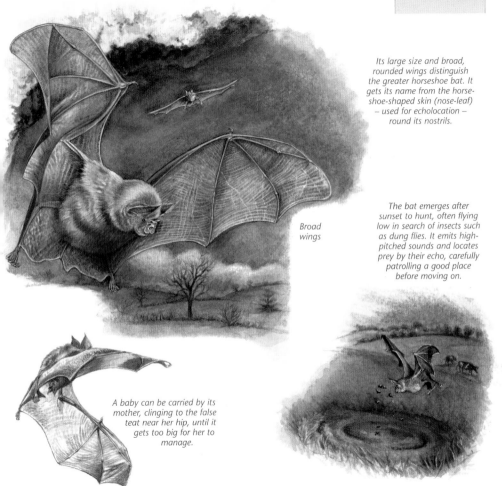

Its large size and broad, rounded wings distinguish the greater horseshoe bat. It gets its name from the horse-shoe-shaped skin (nose-leaf) – used for echolocation – round its nostrils.

Broad wings

The bat emerges after sunset to hunt, often flying low in search of insects such as dung flies. It emits high-pitched sounds and locates prey by their echo, carefully patrolling a good place before moving on.

A baby can be carried by its mother, clinging to the false teat near her hip, until it gets too big for her to manage.

BATS WITH DARK FACES

Pipistrelle
Pipistrellus pipistrellus
Page 190

Tiny: wingspan up to 22cm

Muzzle broad with snub nose. Ears short with a short tragus.

Each tail membrane has a tiny lobe on the edge, just behind heel spur (calcar).

Noctule
Nyctalus noctula
Page 192

Large: wingspan 35cm

Muzzle very broad, bare. Ears rounded with short, semi-circular tragus.

Each tail membrane on the edge, just behind the heel spur (calcar). Leisler's bat similar but smaller and darker.

Muzzle broad. Ears dark with short, pointed tragus.

Tail projects beyond edge of tail membranes.

Serotine
Eptesicus serotinus
Page 194

Large: wingspan 36cm

Whiskered
Myotis mystacinus
Page 202

Muzzle narrow. Ears dark, narrow with a long, pointed tragus.

Small: wingspan 25cm

Tail membranes are straight-edged. Feet tiny with toes almost parallel.

Identifying ordinary bats

THERE ARE ABOUT a dozen species of ordinary bats (bats of the *Vespertilionidae* family) that may be seen in Britain. Most cannot be identified with confidence unless they are closely examined in the hand. Face colour, tail structure and wingspan are the main aids to recognition, also the size, shape and colour of the ears and the size and shape of the tragus – a small, upright projection of skin in the ear. The tragus may be broad, narrow, short or more than three-quarters the length of the ear itself.

Barbastelle
Barbastella barbastellus
Page 198

Muzzle flat. Ears black, broad and squarish, meeting between eyes. Tragus tall, spear-like.

Medium: wingspan 25cm

BATS WITH LIGHT BROWN OR PINKISH FACES

Daubenton's
Myotis daubentoni
Page 203

Medium:
wingspan 25cm

Muzzle broad,
blunt. Ears short, brown,
with narrow, pointed
tragus about half ear length.

Each tail membrane joins
leg half-way up shin. Feet
large with spreading toes.

Long-eared
Plecotus auritus
Page 196

Medium: wingspan 25cm

Muzzle rounded. Ears
very long, oval, joined
at forehead. Tragus
long, narrow, pointed.
Grey species similar
except for colouring.

Natterer's
Myotis nattereri
Page 195

Medium: wingspan 28cm

Muzzle fairly long,
narrow. Ears long,
drooping, each with
long, pointed tragus.
White belly.

Tail membranes baggy with
outward-curving edges and
fringe of fine hairs.

Mouse-eared
Myotis myotis
Page 200

Bechstein's
Myotis bechsteini
Page 201

Muzzle long. Ears long, brownish,
separate at forehead. Tragus
long, pointed.

Muzzle fairly long and narrow.
Ears long, separate at forehead;
droop sideways at rest. Tragus
long and narrow.

Medium: wingspan 28cm

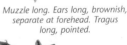

Very large: wingspan 40cm

PIPISTRELLE BATS

THE TINY PIPISTRELLES are Britain's smallest and most abundant bats. Scientists now recognise two species – the common and soprano pipistrelle – but they look almost identical and behave in the same way, living in colonies of 200 or more. Favourite summer roosting places are small, warm spaces behind tiles on a south-facing tile-hung wall, or behind weather-boarding or wooden shingles.

Warmth is essential for the tiny young, born mostly in June. They are hairless for a week after birth and liable to become chilled. In summer, mothers and young live in separate colonies from the males. Winter colonies contain both sexes and it is during winter that mating occurs, although fertilisation is delayed until about April. Pipistrelles hibernate from about late November until late March, preferring cool, dry places such as house roofs or old trees. They fly out sometimes during hibernation, occasionally by day.

Young are born in a large nursery colony, which is often in a roof space behind tiles. They fly after about three weeks.

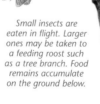

Small insects are eaten in flight. Larger ones may be taken to a feeding roost such as a tree branch. Food remains accumulate on the ground below.

Pipistrelle bat

Pipistrellus pipistrellus
Pipistrellus pygmaeus

35mm; 22cm wingspan

Common. Widespread in all habitats, cities included. May be rare on high ground.

Narrow wings

Short, broad ears

Flight is fast and fluttery with frequent twists and spiral dives as the bats chase prey. They feed mostly on small caddis flies, gnats and tiny moths and are often seen flying low near water.

A mother and baby can fit on a standard-size brick with plenty of room to spare. Young bats have darker fur than adults.

All pipistrelle bats are tiny, but common pipistrelles have darker skin and fur than soprano pipistrelles. The bats often roost in buildings such as churches.

NOCTULE BAT

THE NOCTULE BAT is a powerful flyer, so it is strange that, although common in much of England and Wales, it is not found in Ireland or most of Scotland. It is one of the largest British bats and could easily fly across the Irish Sea.

High-flying noctule bats are often on the wing before dark in summer, swooping after insects among swifts and martins. They are mostly tree dwellers, roosting in colonies in tree holes in parks and woods, although they will sometimes use a house roof. If a roost becomes too hot or too crowded, they move to another.

Like most bats, noctules form nursery roosts of females and young in summer. The young are born in June or July and weaned at about a month old. In winter, from about October until the end of March, the bats hibernate in trees and buildings. They do not use caves, where temperatures are more stable, so hibernating noctules sometimes freeze to death in very cold winters. If they avoid this, and their few predators, they may live for ten years or more.

Noctule bats often live in hollow trees or woodpecker holes. Their short, rounded ears have a rounded tragus (the central lobe in the ear).

Golden-brown fur

Dark brown face

Prey is mostly larger insects caught on the wing. The bat will swoop low to catch an insect such as a cricket.

There is usually only one baby, but females may sometimes have twins.

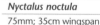

Noctule bat

Nyctalus noctula

75mm; 35cm wingspan

Common in southern Britain, especially in the Midlands and south-eastern counties.

LEISLER'S BAT

Leisler's bat is much like the noctule bat, with short, rounded ears and a broad muzzle. Although it is smaller than the noctule and has slightly darker fur with paler tips, it is hard to tell the two bats apart.

Short, rounded ears

Broad muzzle

Leisler's bat

Nyctalus leisleri

60mm; 30cm wingspan

Patchily distributed. Maybe uncommon. In Ireland it replaces the noctule bat.

In summer adult males gather in small groups and live apart from the females and young.

LEISLER'S BAT, also known as the lesser noctule bat, is very similar to the noctule. It differs only in its smaller size and paler-tipped fur. Both are high flyers, often about before sunset, but have an oddly different distribution. Leisler's bat is found in Ireland, where there are apparently no noctules. But in Britain it has been recorded only rarely, and then in widely separated localities. Like the noctule, Leisler's bat has a short, broad muzzle and a semi-circular tragus (central ear lobe) – features not found in other species of British bats. It is a tree dweller, roosting in tree holes in summer and hibernating in them in winter – from about October until the end of March. Starlings probably deprive Leisler's bats of many roosting holes, which they also have to compete for with the larger noctules. The Leisler's breeding habits are similar to those of noctules. The females each produce one or sometimes two babies a year in June or July, rearing them in nursery roosts. Leisler's bats have few predators and live ten years or more.

SEROTINE BAT

ALTHOUGH A LARGE bat and a strong flyer, the serotine has a surprisingly localised distribution. It is common only in parts of southern and eastern England, especially in the south-east, and where it occurs, it is the large bat most often seen. There are hardly any records of serotine bats being seen to the north or west of the Midlands.

Serotines particularly like to raise their young in the attics of old houses, often hanging up along the roof ridge. Unlike the tiny pipistrelle bat, they are too large to squeeze behind slates and tiles. Colonies may return to the same place year after year, causing an accumulation of small, black droppings in the roof space. Nursing colonies can be noisy and may be unpopular with householders, but it is illegal to disturb them. In any case, once the young are able to look after themselves – usually about August – the colony departs. They spend winter elsewhere, hibernating in another roof or a hollow tree. Serotines probably live for about five years. Some may survive to be 15 or more.

Young are born singly. A mother can carry a small, pink baby clinging to her body if the nursery roost is disturbed. An adult's tail tip projects noticeably beyond the edge of the tail membrane.

The bat crawls with forewings folded, hooking its thumbs on a rough surface while it pushes with its hind feet.

Slow-flying serotine bats eat mostly large moths and beetles, caught on the wing.

Serotine bat

Eptesicus serotinus

64mm; 36cm wingspan

Common in parts of southern and eastern England. A few isolated sightings in north.

Grizzled
brown fur

The serotine is a large
bat with powerful jaws,
a dark face and ears and a
pointed tragus (the central
lobe in the ear).

Dark face
and ears

The bats emerge
shortly after sunset
and are high flyers. They
are large bats, but seem
even bigger and heavier
in the failing light.

The gable end of a brick house with a
slate roof is a typical site for a nursery
colony, often numbering 50-100 bats.

COMMON LONG-EARED BAT

ALL BRITISH BATS use their hearing to navigate and to locate food. They emit sound pulses – too high-pitched for human ears – that reflect from obstacles, including tiny insects. These echoes enable all bats to locate flying insects, but the huge, extra-sensitive ears of the long-eared bat can also detect insects perched on leaves, and even distinguish between an adult insect and a larva such as a caterpillar.

The long-eared bat can also fly with fine control in small spaces, threading through tree branches and foliage and even hovering above a leaf to pick off an insect. It is mainly a woodland bat that roosts in trees, although it often breeds in attics. Long-eared bats hibernate, usually alone, from about November to March, perhaps in a cave or mine, but also sometimes in the summer roost, which is unusual among bats. Some live for 12 years or more. The common long-eared bat differs from the rare grey long-eared bat in colour. It has yellowish-tipped pale brown fur, whereas the grey has darker fur with hairs dark grey at the base.

Unlike other bats, the long-eared bat feeds extensively on insects or larvae resting on foliage. It hovers while it seizes prey.

To reduce loss of moisture when hibernating, the bat folds its ears back alongside the body and tucks them under the wings. The tragus, a spear-like central lobe in the ear, remains hanging down.

Common long-eared bat

Plecotus auritus

45mm; 25cm wingspan

Found in woods, house roofs. Widespread, but not in open, exposed places or far north.

Huge oval ears meeting at the base distinguish the long-eared bat. The ears are about 28mm long, nearly three-quarters of the length of the head and body.

Yellowy-brown fur

Broad wings

Grey long-eared bat
Plecotus austriacus

The bat flies with ears erect. Its broad, rounded wings allow slow flight and easy movement in small spaces. It can hover with its body almost upright.

It is difficult to tell the difference between the grey and common long-eared bats. The grey is slightly larger and has greyer, darker fur. It is rare in Britain, but widespread on the Continent. A few are found in the south in Dorset and Hampshire.

BARBASTELLE BAT

NO OTHER BRITISH BAT bears any resemblance to the strange-looking barbastelle, with its squashed face, thick black ears that meet between the eyes and long, frosted-looking, blackish fur. It is so peculiar that there is only one other species like it in the world, another barbastelle of the Middle East and Asia.

Despite their distinctive looks, barbastelles are rarely sighted. They are found in open woodland, especially in river valleys, where they fly low over the water and are active intermittently through the night. As with all bats, the males are smaller than the females and tend to be solitary, leaving the females to form nursery colonies in summer to raise the young. In winter, barbastelles have been found hibernating in caves and grottoes with other bats, but only in the coldest weather. They tend to choose the coolest places to hibernate, which suggests that they can tolerate low temperatures and spend winter in relatively unsheltered sites. The bat can live for at least 18 years.

Short broad ears

Glossy, almost black fur, with frosted look on older bats.

The distinctive barbastelle bat has a pug-like face with a bare, dark brown snout and short, broad ears that meet between the eyes.

The ears are almost as broad as they are long, and have a stiffening fold at the front. There is a long, pointed tragus (central ear lobe).

Although a barbastelle usually alights head up, it may twist round before attaching itself to hang head down from a wall or tree trunk.

Barbastelle bat

Barbastella barbastellus

50mm; 27cm wingspan

Found only in the southern half of Britain, but elusive and rarely seen.

NATTERER'S BAT

NAMED AFTER its discoverer, Johann Natterer, an early 19th-century Austrian naturalist, the bat is most easily recognised by its pure white underside as it flies slowly and often at rooftop height soon after sunset, searching for small flying insects such as moths. In flight the bat often holds its tail pointing down instead of trailing to the rear, as is usual in other bats. Along the edge of each tail membrane there are about ten tiny, bead-like swellings, each sprouting a short, fine, scarcely visible hair. The function of this fringe, unique among bats, is unknown. In summer, breeding colonies of females and young gather in hollow trees or house roofs. The females bear only one baby in June or early July. It can fly by about August. During their first year, young Natterer's bats can be distinguished from adults by their greyish-brown colouring. The bats hibernate from about December to early March in caves, or other sites such as hollow trees. They can live for 25 years.

Natterer's bat has a pure white underside, and its tail membranes are baggy with outward-curving edges. Its face is long and reddish with a bare, narrow muzzle.

Natterer's bat

Myotis nattereri

45mm; 28cm wingspan

Common. Widespread in woods, farmland and parkland. Not found in northern Scotland.

The ears droop sideways and have distinct upturned tips, which are darker than the pinkish bases. If laid forwards they extend well beyond the bat's nostrils.

When the bat crawls, the dividing line between its light brown upper parts and white underside shows clearly.

MOUSE-EARED BAT

ITS SLOW, HEAVY flight and large wingspan – almost a third larger than that of any other British species – easily distinguishes the mouse-eared bat. It is the biggest bat known in Britain, but, despite legal protection since 1975, may now be extinct.

The only known regular haunts have been in Dorset and Sussex, and these bats may have flown across the Channel from France, a short journey well worth the effort for a mouse-eared bat seeking a suitable place to spend winter. In eastern Europe mouse-eared bats are known to travel 200km or more between their summer and winter quarters. Mouse-eared bats seem to prefer open woodland or farming country. In summer the females give birth to their single young in a warm, dry place such as an attic, and the males live alone elsewhere. Winter is often spent in the cool, sheltered conditions of a cave or an old mine tunnel. The bats can live for 15 years or more.

Grey-brown back

Wide wingspan

Britain's biggest bat, the mouse-eared bat is distinguished by its wide wingspan, bare, pinkish face and large, wide ears.

Large ears

Greyish-white underparts

A nursery roost may be in a warm dry attic or an old railway tunnel.

When the bat crawls, the sharp dividing line between its body colours shows clearly.

Mouse-eared bat

Myotis myotis

70mm; 40cm wingspan

Some colonies recorded in Dorset and Sussex, but probably now extinct in Britain.

BECHSTEIN'S BAT

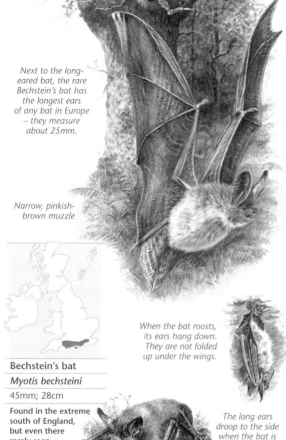

Next to the long-eared bat, the rare Bechstein's bat has the longest ears of any bat in Europe – they measure about 25mm.

Narrow, pinkish-brown muzzle

Bechstein's bat

Myotis bechsteini

45mm; 28cm

Found in the extreme south of England, but even there rarely seen.

When the bat roosts, its ears hang down. They are not folded up under the wings.

The long ears droop to the side when the bat is at rest. The ears do not meet at their bases like a long-eared bat's.

THE ELUSIVE BECHSTEIN'S bat is one of Britain's rarest mammals. Only a few dozen sightings have ever been made, mostly in Dorset, where the bat, with its distinctive long ears, hibernates in old limestone mines along with several other species. The bat ranges throughout Europe but is very scarce there too. Most sightings have been in Germany, and the bat is named after Johann Bechstein, an early 19th-century German naturalist. It was first discovered on the Continent and only later found to occur in Britain. Bechstein's bat seems to be a woodland species that frequents parkland, often flying about 3m above the ground, and roosts in hollow trees. Its bones have been found in old flint mines that date back to the Stone Age, when most of southern Britain was covered by extensive forests. Like other bats, female Bechstein's bats give birth to one baby a year. The nursery roost is often in an attic or tree hole. The bat probably feeds mostly on moths, sometimes other insects, taking them mainly in flight but also off leaves.

WHISKERED BAT

Narrow, pointed wings

Tiny feet

DESPITE ITS NAME, the whiskered bat does not have particularly prominent whiskers, but it does have more fur round the eyes and muzzle than most other bats. It is very similar to another species, Brandt's bat, and in fact the two are so alike that they were only recognised as separate species in 1970. Even experts find them hard to tell apart. Common around buildings, hedges or woodland fringes, they may be seen from early evening as they make slow, fluttering flights in search of insects. Usually they follow a regular track repeatedly before moving on.

Both species hibernate in cool spots from late autumn. Mating occurs during short periods of wakefulness in winter, so the females are pregnant as soon as (or soon after) they emerge in early spring, allowing the single young to be born early in summer, usually about June. They then have time to feed, grow and fatten up before winter, when food becomes insufficient for normal activity. The bats can live for about 19 years.

These bats are small and delicate. The muzzle is narrow and the face and ears very dark, especially in young animals in their first year which also have darker underparts than adults.

The pointed, upright ears give these bats a rather perky look. The tragus (central ear lobe) is narrow and pointed.

Whiskered bat
Brandt's bat

Myotis mystacinus
Myotis brandtii

40mm; 25cm wingspan

Both widespread except in far north. Probably found in Ireland, but not recorded.

DAUBENTON'S BAT

WHEN IT SKIMS over a pond or lake at night, Daubenton's bat uses shallow, fluttering wing beats to get close to the surface. In this way it can pick up mayflies as they emerge from the water, and also catch other aquatic insects, plankton and even small fish – a food source not exploited by other British bats. It does not always hunt low, and may be seen flying fairly high. Daubenton's bat is widespread and usually found not far from trees or water. When hunting, a Daubenton's bat often patrols repeatedly up and down a regular beat, then moves to another. These favoured beats may actually be defended from other bats, but little is known of bats' territorial and social behaviour because of the difficulty of studying them in flight and in the dark. Daubenton's females bear one baby a year about June or July. Nursery roosts, with no adult males present, are often in buildings and may contain scores of bats. During winter, the bats tend to be solitary, hibernating alone in caves or trees.

Daubenton's bat is often called the water bat because of its tendency to fly very low over water. It has short ears and a short, broad, pinkish-brown muzzle. The large feet with splayed toes are distinctive.

Daubenton's bat

Myotis daubentoni

45mm; 25cm

Widespread in most parts of Britain except exposed places.

To hibernate, a bat may crawl backwards into a crevice in a cave, wall, rock face or hollow tree.

The bat's short ears are wider than those of the whiskered bat, and paler at the base.

3 Many kinds of bat like to roost or hibernate in old trees. As these fall or are cut down, bats have fewer places to live.

1 Caves provide sheltered, humid places in which bats can hibernate during winter. Horseshoe bats especially may travel long distances to find a suitable cave. Many caves are now blocked up.

2 Many bats like to live in woodland. But conifer plantations, which have dense stands of trees of the same age, support fewer insects and lack holes where bats can roost.

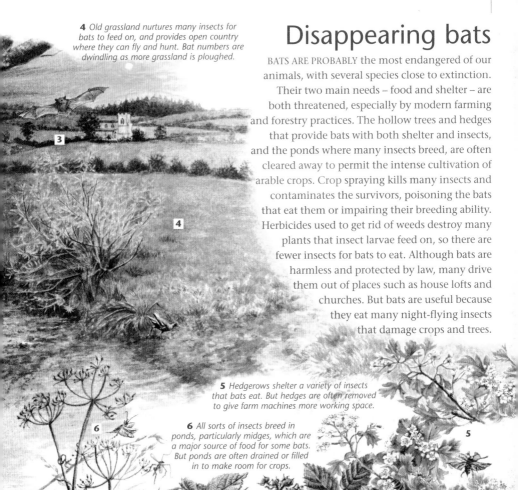

Disappearing bats

4 *Old grassland nurtures many insects for bats to feed on, and provides open country where they can fly and hunt. Bat numbers are dwindling as more grassland is ploughed.*

BATS ARE PROBABLY the most endangered of our animals, with several species close to extinction. Their two main needs – food and shelter – are both threatened, especially by modern farming and forestry practices. The hollow trees and hedges that provide bats with both shelter and insects, and the ponds where many insects breed, are often cleared away to permit the intense cultivation of arable crops. Crop spraying kills many insects and contaminates the survivors, poisoning the bats that eat them or impairing their breeding ability. Herbicides used to get rid of weeds destroy many plants that insect larvae feed on, so there are fewer insects for bats to eat. Although bats are harmless and protected by law, many drive them out of places such as house lofts and churches. But bats are useful because they eat many night-flying insects that damage crops and trees.

5 *Hedgerows shelter a variety of insects that bats eat. But hedges are often removed to give farm machines more working space.*

6 *All sorts of insects breed in ponds, particularly midges, which are a major source of food for some bats. But ponds are often drained or filled in to make room for crops.*

COMMON FROG

OPEN WOODS and lush pastures are typically the home of the common frog, which likes moist places not too far from water. But frogs are becoming increasingly common in gardens with ponds, and it is not unusual to find a hundred or more using a pond for spawning. As frogs eat insects and small animals such as slugs and snails, they are good friends to the gardener. They like to hide in tall vegetation on summer days, and emerge on warm damp nights to hunt.

From about mid October, common frogs hibernate in sheltered places on land or in the muddy bottoms of ponds. They emerge to migrate to breeding ponds, usually in February or March, but as early as January in the south-west. After spawning frogs usually stay in the water until the weather gets warmer, leaving during April to live on land. When the young frogs emerge in June or July, large numbers are killed by predators such as blackbirds. At any age they may fall prey to many animals, including herons, hedgehogs, rats, foxes and cats.

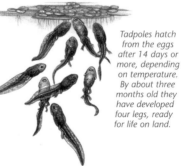

Frogs go to the same breeding place year after year. Because many natural ponds have become polluted or been drained, the commonest breeding places are now artificial garden ponds.

The eggs (spawn) are laid in a mass in a transparent jelly that protects the embryo frogs and also keeps them slightly warm, so speeding development.

Tadpoles hatch from the eggs after 14 days or more, depending on temperature. By about three months old they have developed four legs, ready for life on land.

Common frog

Rana temporaria

75mm

Widespread in wet habitats, but land drainage is making it locally extinct.

Dark patch behind eye

Variable skin colour

The common frog lives on land in damp places for most of the year, often blending well with its surroundings. Body colour varies widely from dark greenish-grey to chestnut or yellow, or sometimes albino. Female is slightly larger than male.

When young frogs first leave the water, usually during June, they still have a stumpy tadpole tail, but this soon disappears.

Frogs move by hopping or leaping; they do not crawl. Their long hind legs enable them to leap up to 50cm from a standing start.

MARSH FROG

EUROPE'S LARGEST FROG, the marsh frog was introduced to Britain from Hungary in 1935 by a zoologist, Percy Smith. He released some in his garden at Stone-in-Oxney, on the border of Romney Marsh, and they spread to the drainage dykes and ditches that criss-cross the marsh. They are now found in adjoining areas of Kent and Sussex, but attempts to introduce them to other counties have not succeeded.

Marsh frogs like to bask in the sun, but, if disturbed, take to the water. They feed mostly on land, mainly eating flying insects. At breeding time from early April to June, the males gather in the water in small groups and croak loudly, distending their vocal sacs, as they call to attract females. The spawn is deposited in small clumps among waterweed, and the tadpoles are rarely seen. Young frogs emerge from the water in September and October. A change from sheep to arable farming on Romney Marsh is altering the dyke system and may affect the marsh frog's survival.

Drainage dykes are the home of the marsh frog, which catches most of its food on land. The frogs breed in a dyke or at the edge of a large pool in late April, May and June.

In April marsh frogs emerge from the water after hibernating in the mud or stones at the bottom of a pond. They do not mate until a few weeks later.

Food is caught on the frog's sticky tongue. It feeds on insects such as mayflies and other small creatures such as worms.

Marsh frog

Rana ridibunda

10cm

Found in drainage dykes and ditches only in Romney Marsh and the surrounding area.

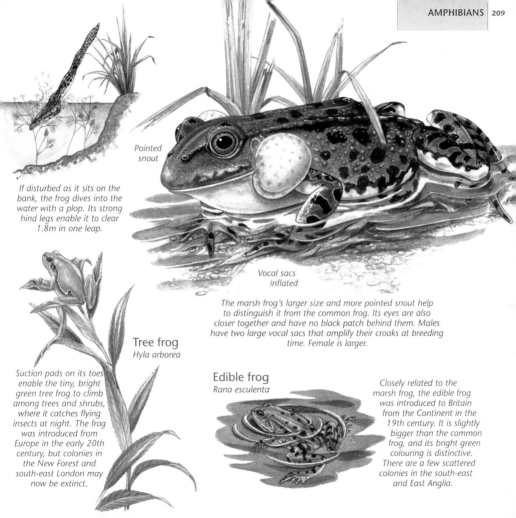

If disturbed as it sits on the bank, the frog dives into the water with a plop. Its strong hind legs enable it to clear 1.8m in one leap.

Pointed snout

Vocal sacs inflated

The marsh frog's larger size and more pointed snout help to distinguish it from the common frog. Its eyes are also closer together and have no black patch behind them. Males have two large vocal sacs that amplify their croaks at breeding time. Female is larger.

Tree frog
Hyla arborea

Suction pads on its toes enable the tiny, bright green tree frog to climb among trees and shrubs, where it catches flying insects at night. The frog was introduced from Europe in the early 20th century, but colonies in the New Forest and south-east London may now be extinct.

Edible frog
Rana esculenta

Closely related to the marsh frog, the edible frog was introduced to Britain from the Continent in the 19th century. It is slightly bigger than the common frog, and its bright green colouring is distinctive. There are a few scattered colonies in the south-east and East Anglia.

COMMON TOAD

TOAD MIGRATION in March or early April can be spectacular. In the space of a few days, hundreds of common toads leave their hibernation places and head for breeding ponds, climbing walls and other obstacles and crossing roads. Many are killed, especially by vehicles.

Common toads like to spawn in fairly deep water. Strings of spawn are usually about 2-3m long. Eggs develop into tadpoles and then young toads in about 10-16 weeks. Young toads leave the water in June or July, only 1 in 20 surviving to become adult. Males are ready to breed at about three years old and females a year later, so males outnumber females at breeding time.

When spawning is over, adults leave the ponds to live alone throughout summer. Most of the day is spent under logs, but the toads emerge in the evening to catch insects and other small animals. They sit and wait for prey to come within range of their long tongue, rooted at the front of the mouth. In captivity toads may live for 20 years, but in the wild not usually more than ten.

In winter, from about mid October to mid March, toads hibernate under logs or stones, singly or in large groups. They usually find dry places not far from their breeding ponds.

At night a toad's eyes have large, circular pupils. In daylight the pupils contract to slits bordered by a golden iris. Toads walk, they do not leap as frogs do, and are slow and clumsy in comparison.

Every spring toads migrate to regularly used breeding ponds for spawning. Males emit sharp croaks and clasp females tightly from behind, fertilising spawn as it is laid in long strings that wrap round water plants.

Common toad
Bufo bufo
10cm
Common and widespread, but not in Ireland. Frequent in gardens, often in dry places.

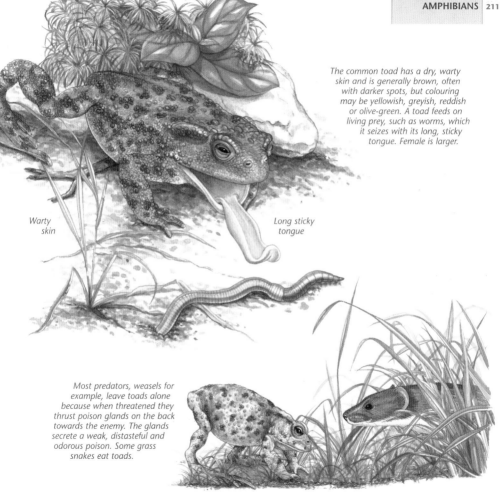

The common toad has a dry, warty skin and is generally brown, often with darker spots, but colouring may be yellowish, greyish, reddish or olive-green. A toad feeds on living prey, such as worms, which it seizes with its long, sticky tongue. Female is larger.

Warty skin

Long sticky tongue

Most predators, weasels for example, leave toads alone because when threatened they thrust poison glands on the back towards the enemy. The glands secrete a weak, distasteful and odorous poison. Some grass snakes eat toads.

NATTERJACK TOAD

THE NAME OF THE natterjack toad is probably derived from the Anglo-Saxon word *naeddre*, meaning a serpent or crawling creature. The addition of 'jack' may refer to the toad's small size, as it does in jacksnipe, for instance. The toad is found only in sandy places, mainly in dunes in East Anglia and the north-west, but was once common on southern heaths. Now its numbers are declining and it is protected by law.

Natterjack toads dig burrows in soft sand, often sheltering there in a group. They emerge to forage at night, feeding on insects and other small animals. Winter is spent buried 30-60cm deep in the sand. Spawning begins in April and continues until June or July. During this time the males sit in the water round the edges of the shallow, sandy pools used for breeding and croak loudly. Their night chorus may be heard more than 2km away. Many tadpoles die when their ponds dry up before they become toadlets. Most toadlets leave the water in June or July. Toads may live 10-12 years.

The spawn is laid in strings about 1-2m long in shallow water, wrapped round plants. The strands have single rows of black eggs, not double rows like common toad spawn.

A burrowing toad digs with its forelimbs, throwing soil behind as a dog would do.

Because its hind legs are shorter than those of the common toad, the natterjack can crawl faster. It is often active in daylight.

Natterjack toad

Bufo calamita

64mm

Found on sandy heaths and coastal dunes. Common in a few restricted localities.

When frightened,
the natterjack, like the
common toad, adopts a
defensive posture. It arches its
back towards an attacker so that
the poison-secreting glands on its
back are uppermost.

A yellow line down the middle of its
back distinguishes the natterjack
toad from the common toad. It is
also slightly smaller and has a
shinier, smoother skin. Adults
vary in colour from yellowish-
green to olive-green.

Midwife toad
Alytes obstetricans

At breeding time, from March to
midsummer, males call loudly to attract
females. Each distends its single throat sac
to give a penetrating, rattling croak.

For a few weeks in late spring and
early summer, a male midwife toad
carries eggs from the female twined
round its back and hind legs. It takes
them to water when they are ready to
hatch. One small colony is known in
Britain, accidentally introduced in
the 1800s with water plants.

COMMON NEWT

ALTHOUGH COMMON NEWTS live in their breeding pools for most of spring, they spend summer and autumn on land. Most newts also hibernate on land during winter. Open woodland and scrub or lush pasture, with breeding ponds nearby, are typical places for newts, and they are becoming common in gardens. By day they hide under stones or logs or in thick grass, emerging on damp nights to hunt for slugs, worms and insects, tracking prey by both sight and scent. Newts look a little like lizards but have no scales, move slowly and never bask in the sun.

Early in spring newts move to the water to breed. Each egg is wrapped in a water plant leaf. Adults return to land in early summer, leaving the tadpoles to develop into fully formed but tiny newts which emerge to live on land at the end of summer. They stay there until two years old, then return to the water to breed. Common newts are the most abundant species. If it escapes predators such as hedgehogs, rats and grass snakes, a newt can live about ten years.

At breeding time male common newts have a bright orange underside and spots on the throat as well as the belly. Male palmate newts have a whitish-yellow underside and plain pink throat. The females of the two species are drabber and hard to tell apart.

The tiny young leave the water at the end of summer, after they have changed from tadpoles into miniature newts.

Like all newts, common newts are greedy feeders. With their sticky tongues they catch slugs, worms, insects and even other newts. They swallow their prey whole – including snails in their shells.

Common newt

Triturus vulgaris

10cm

Common, widespread, mainly in lowland Britain. The only newt found in Ireland.

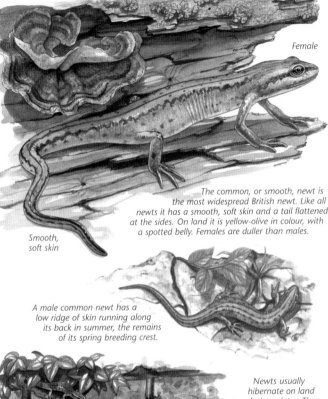

Female

The common, or smooth, newt is the most widespread British newt. Like all newts it has a smooth, soft skin and a tail flattened at the sides. On land it is yellow-olive in colour, with a spotted belly. Females are duller than males.

Smooth, soft skin

A male common newt has a low ridge of skin running along its back in summer, the remains of its spring breeding crest.

Newts usually hibernate on land during winter. They often choose a damp cellar or a garden corner, but are never far from water.

Great crested newt
Triturus cristatus

The largest British newt, with a slimy, warty skin, blackish above with a black-spotted golden-yellow belly. Males have a high, toothed crest and a silver-streaked tail. The species is declining and is protected by law. About 16cm long including tail.

Palmate newt
Triturus helveticus

The smallest British newt, olive-brown above with a dark streak across the eye. Breeding males have webbed hind feet, a low, smooth crest and a short filament on the tail. About 75mm long including tail.

A garden pond

GARDEN PONDS have become lifesavers for Britain's frogs, toads and newts in the past 50 years, as farm and village ponds are filled in or become polluted. They also benefit the gardener as the amphibians they attract prey on pests such as slugs and snails.

Whether made from an old sink or a plastic liner, a pond is soon colonised by insects such as pond skaters. A few jars of pond water tipped in will add plankton, pond snails and other food sources for larger creatures such as water beetles. Frogs and toads may arrive of their own accord, but a colony can be started by introducing spawn in spring and leaving it to develop. If all goes well, adults will return to breed two or three years later. Toads generally prefer deeper ponds than frogs. Newts may find their own way, or can be caught as adults (but not the protected great crested newt) and released in the pond in spring.

1 Long, damp grass near the pond provides shelter for young frogs, which leave the water in June or July.

2 Newts spend most of the year on land in damp places – under logs, for example. They hunt for prey such as slugs at night.

3 Birds often drink or bathe in shallow garden ponds. Blackbirds will also feed on tadpoles.

4 Frogs like shallow water, about 10cm deep, for spawning in February or March. They spend the rest of the year in damp places near the water.

5 In a shallow corner the water gets warmer and speeds tadpole development. If there are goldfish in the pond, they will eat large numbers of tadpoles.

6 A rockery or a rough brick wall provides crevices for frogs, newts and toads to hide in by day. Plenty of undergrowth, will also encourage small mammals such as bank voles and wood mice to move in.

ADDER

LEGEND SAYS that a female adder in danger swallows her young. In reality, the young snakes are hiding under their mother's belly. The adder, or viper, is the most widespread snake in Britain and the only poisonous one. But it is timid and normally flees from humans before they get close enough to provoke it. The bite is rarely fatal.

Adders like open places such as heaths, moors and hillsides, and sometimes sanddunes. They shed their skins from time to time, and cast skins may be a sign of their presence. Adders eat small mammals such as mice, voles and shrews as well as nestling birds, lizards, frogs and toads, but not every day – a big meal may last a week or more. Male adders emerge from hibernation in February or March, females a little later, and courtship reaches a peak in April. Females usually become pregnant only once every two years. The young are born fully formed in August or September and take three or four years to reach maturity. Adders have few enemies apart from man, and may live for nine or ten years.

Adders usually hunt by day. They kill with a bite from hollow, hinged fangs, which inject poison from venom glands in the upper jaw. If the victim does not die at once, the adder trails it, using its forked tongue to follow the scent.

Females are duller, browner and fatter than males, with less contrast between markings and background colouring. They usually have up to 15 young at a time. Although young adders sometimes hide under their mother, she gives them no parental care and they disperse soon after birth.

Adder

Vipera berus

60-76cm

Widespread, but distribution patchy. Found in hedgerows, farmland, open moors and woods.

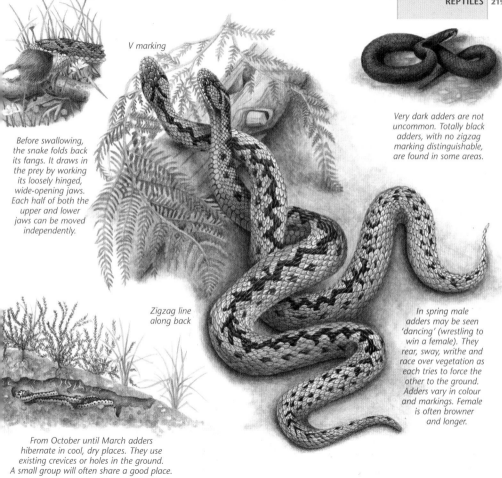

V marking

Before swallowing, the snake folds back its fangs. It draws in the prey by working its loosely hinged, wide-opening jaws. Each half of both the upper and lower jaws can be moved independently.

Very dark adders are not uncommon. Totally black adders, with no zigzag marking distinguishable, are found in some areas.

Zigzag line along back

In spring male adders may be seen 'dancing' (wrestling to win a female). They rear, sway, writhe and race over vegetation as each tries to force the other to the ground. Adders vary in colour and markings. Female is often browner and longer.

From October until March adders hibernate in cool, dry places. They use existing crevices or holes in the ground. A small group will often share a good place.

SMOOTH SNAKE

THE LOWLAND HEATHS of Hampshire, Dorset and Surrey are the home of the smooth snake, one of Britain's rarest animals. The snake is protected by law, but its survival depends on preserving heathland under increasing pressure from farmers and foresters, walkers and picnickers, and heath fires.

Because the smooth snake is shy as well as rare, much is still to be learned about its way of life. It rarely basks in the open, preferring to get the sun's warmth indirectly by lying under a flat stone or similar object. In spring, when they emerge from hibernation, smooth snakes are sometimes seen basking intertwined in heather. Individuals have a home range that they keep to for long periods. Much of their time is spent burrowing underground, and they mostly eat other reptiles such as lizards. Mating takes place in May. The young are born in August or September and are self-sufficient from birth. The snakes may survive in the wild for 15-20 years or more.

The snake is not poisonous. It holds its prey in its coiled body while it gets into position to swallow the victim head first. The smooth snake preys on lizards and will also eat small mammals. Young snakes eat insects and spiders.

Up to 15 young are born at a time, each within a thin membrane that ruptures at once. They are about 15cm long, with darker heads and spots than adults.

Like all snakes, the smooth snake is brightest in colour after shedding its skin. Old skin is regularly cast off in one piece, the snake squeezing between roots and twigs to free it.

Smooth snake

Coronella austriaca

60cm

Very rare. Found on some heaths in south of England. Numbers probably declining.

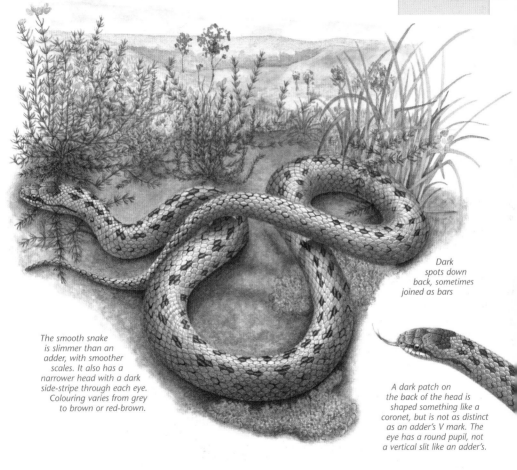

Dark spots down back, sometimes joined as bars

The smooth snake is slimmer than an adder, with smoother scales. It also has a narrower head with a dark side-stripe through each eye. Colouring varies from grey to brown or red-brown.

A dark patch on the back of the head is shaped something like a coronet, but is not as distinct as an adder's V mark. The eye has a round pupil, not a vertical slit like an adder's.

GRASS SNAKE

A grass snake swims with sinuous body movements as it hunts in a pond or a stream. It swallows tadpoles underwater but takes larger prey ashore to eat.

DAMP GRASS, ditches, pond banks and slow-moving streams are likely haunts for the harmless grass snake, Britain's largest snake. It feeds on amphibians such as frogs, and a large meal will satisfy it for a week or ten days. Like other reptiles, they spend a lot of time basking in the spring sun after emerging from hibernation in April. Courting and mating follow soon after.

The grass snake lays its eggs in a place where heat is generated, such as a compost heap. A female will travel up to 2km to find a suitable site, where hundreds of eggs may be laid by June or July, hatching in August or September. The young enjoy the summer sun while growing, giving them energy to hunt and fatten up for winter. Hibernation, perhaps in wall crevices or under tree roots, begins in October. Snakes not taken by birds, hedgehogs or badgers may live about nine years.

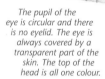

The pupil of the eye is circular and there is no eyelid. The eye is always covered by a transparent part of the skin. The top of the head is all one colour.

To lay her eggs, the female burrows into a place where heat is generated, such as a haystack, a manure heap or rotting vegetation. The eggs, up to 40, are matt white and 30mm long.

The eggs, held in clusters by a sticky film, have flexible shells. Two months after laying, young snakes about 19cm emerge through slits made by an eggtooth on the snout. The tooth is then shed.

Grass snake

Natrix natrix

120cm

Commonest in lowland areas. Found mainly in damp heaths, woods, or in lush pastures.

As with all snakes, each scale on the underside spans the body width. Scales have sharp rear edges and dig into the ground to give the snake a grip as it moves forward.

Black dots along greenish back

Black bars on flanks

Also known as the ringed snake, the grass snake has two yellow or white patches almost encircling its neck. The belly is patterned with black, grey and white. Females are bigger than males.

Neck patches

A snake's skin is shed 3-12 times a year. Before shedding, it goes dull and dark and the snake's eyes look misty. Colouring is brightest just after shedding.

When threatened by a predator, a grass snake sometimes feigns death by lying on its back with its tongue lolling. It may eject smelly liquid.

COMMON LIZARD

RUSTLES IN THE undergrowth may be the first sign of a common lizard's presence as it nimbly scampers up a bank to hide. Lizards live on heathland, sanddunes, grass or scrub-covered banks and on high moors, forming large colonies where conditions are ideal. They emerge from hibernation early in spring, at first basking in the sun but less so as the weather gets warmer. They court and mate in April and the young are born in midsummer. Before autumn ends the lizards retire into cracks and under stones to hibernate.

Common lizards eat a variety of small creatures, spiders particularly, which they hunt throughout warm days. At night and on cool days they remain hidden. Lizards themselves fall prey to many animals, including smooth snakes, adders, rats and birds – particularly kestrels. If a predator seizes a lizard's tail, it can shed it and so escape; the tail may even be shed if the lizard is merely threatened. A new tail grows from the stump, but is never as long or as perfect as the original.

The transparent surface layer of skin is shed periodically. It is scraped off in pieces, making the lizard look ragged until moulting is completed.

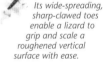

Its wide-spreading, sharp-clawed toes enable a lizard to grip and scale a roughened vertical surface with ease.

There are usually five to eight black young – sometimes ten – born fully formed, each in a transparent capsule that breaks at birth. They may all be born at once, or over a one or two-day period. Common lizards may live for five or six years.

Common lizard

Lacerta vivipara

15cm

Widespread in open places throughout Britain. The only lizard in Scotland and Ireland.

A male's underside is usually orange with black spots, a female's lemon-yellow with no spots. Lizards have rows of scales across the underside, not single scales like snakes.

Male

Female

Male

Female

Dull brown is the typical lizard colouring, but it may be tinged red, yellow, grey or green. There is almost always a dark back stripe, and often dark side stripes with white edges. Stripes are sometimes broken. The female is fatter than the male and usually paler.

A lizard may be seen with a short tail as it grows a replacement for one that has been shed. Sometimes a new tail grows beside one only partly lost, giving a double tail.

Spiders, harvestmen, flies and beetles are among the lizard's prey. It catches prey in its jaws and shakes and stuns it before eating.

SAND LIZARD

DRY, OPEN COUNTRY is the home of the sand lizard, chiefly the sandy heaths of Surrey, Hampshire and Dorset, though a small population lives on the coastal dunes near Liverpool. As the heaths give way to farming and forestry and the sanddunes become less secluded, sand lizards have become scarce. They are now protected by law.

The sand lizard emerges from its hibernating burrow, deep in the sand, in March or April, then basks and sheds its old skin. Males emerge first, their dull winter colours soon replaced by emerald-green flanks. In April and May the males fight for dominance, the victors pairing up with females. Adult lizards feed well in summer, mainly on large insects such as grasshoppers and beetles, to build up fat reserves for winter. They may hibernate as early as the end of August. Young lizards hatch in late August or September and grow rapidly before hibernating in October. Sand lizards need at least two years to mature and may live to seven or eight.

In late May or June the female digs a hole in a sunny place in soft sand, lays her eggs there and covers them up.

The oval eggs, about 13mm long, hatch after two or three months. The newly hatched lizards are 64mm long.

Young sand lizards can be distinguished from common lizards by their more conspicuous spots.

In the April-June breeding season adult males threaten each other and pick fights. One may display its conspicuous flank colouring to intimidate an opponent.

Sand lizard

Lacerta agilis

18cm

In the north-west of England prefers coastal dunes, but in the south sandy heaths.

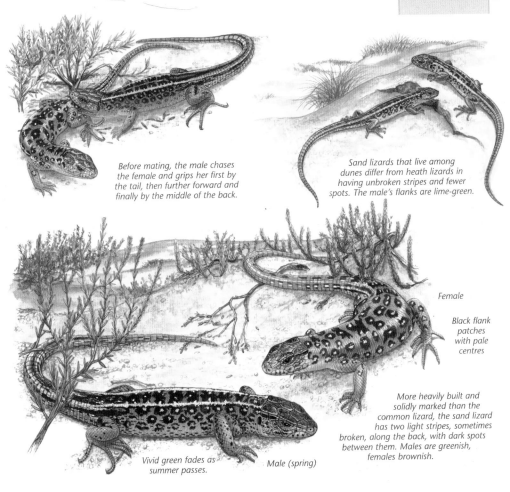

Before mating, the male chases the female and grips her first by the tail, then further forward and finally by the middle of the back.

Sand lizards that live among dunes differ from heath lizards in having unbroken stripes and fewer spots. The male's flanks are lime-green.

Female

Black flank patches with pale centres

More heavily built and solidly marked than the common lizard, the sand lizard has two light stripes, sometimes broken, along the back, with dark spots between them. Males are greenish, females brownish.

Vivid green fades as summer passes.

Male (spring)

SLOW-WORM

AT ONE TIME any creeping, serpent-like animal was called a worm, which is how the slow-worm – or blind-worm – got its name. It is in fact a legless lizard but is often mistaken for a snake and killed, though harmless. As slug-eaters, slow-worms are an asset to any garden. They move slowly and deliberately, but can move fast if disturbed.

Slow-worms live on sunny banks and hillsides with cover such as grass, scrub or stones. Pieces of their shed skins may be left behind. Hibernation underground begins in October and ends in March, when slow-worms emerge to bask in the early spring sun. Mating takes place in April and May, when males may fight, seizing and sometimes biting each other on or near the head. From 6 to 12 young are born in August or September or, more rarely, in the following spring.

Slow-worms take about three years to mature and can then live longer than any other lizards; one in captivity has reached its fifties. Such an age is unlikely in the wild, where enemies include hedgehogs, rats and kestrels.

Each young slow-worm is born in a membranous egg that it breaks open within seconds. It is golden-yellow above and black below, and 75mm long.

Much of the slow-worm's time is spent underground. It burrows in soft soil, such as a garden compost heap. Although often found in an ants' nest, it does not often eat them.

Slow-worm

Anguis fragilis

45cm

Widespread and common but shy and not often seen. Rarely basks in the open.

Like most lizards, the slow-worm has eyelids and can close its eyes, and also has a broad, flat tongue. But it differs in having no visible earholes.

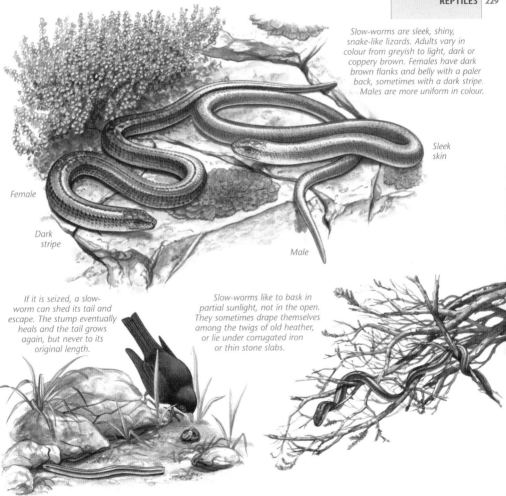

Slow-worms are sleek, shiny, snake-like lizards. Adults vary in colour from greyish to light, dark or coppery brown. Females have dark brown flanks and belly with a paler back, sometimes with a dark stripe. Males are more uniform in colour.

Sleek skin

Female

Dark stripe

Male

If it is seized, a slow-worm can shed its tail and escape. The stump eventually heals and the tail grows again, but never to its original length.

Slow-worms like to bask in partial sunlight, not in the open. They sometimes drape themselves among the twigs of old heather, or lie under corrugated iron or thin stone slabs.

1 A common lizard keeps its body heat at about 30°C for as long as it can by basking in the sun and cooling in the shade. In weak sun it flattens its body to expose as much to the sun as possible. On hot days it turns its face to the sun, so offering a smaller surface to receive warmth. Basking exposes the lizard to kestrels and crows; it always has to be ready to dart into a crevice.

2 Pieces of corrugated iron and other metal, such as farm machinery and garden tools, become very warm in the sun and reptiles can bask under them secure from attack.

3 Slow-worms bask in semi-shaded places such as in long grass or the shadow of a wall. They absorb less warmth there but are less visible to predators.

4 *A crevice in a dry-stone wall or a burrow at its base offers a common lizard a place to hide at night and on sunless days, as well as somewhere to hibernate from October to March.*

Basking in the sun

ALTHOUGH REPTILES such as snakes and lizards are usually described as coldblooded, they spend much of their lives with their bodies nearly as warm as in a warm-blooded animal. What they lack is a means of producing and maintaining their own body heat. To reach a body temperature at which muscles, senses and digestion are fully active (about 25-32°C), they have to rely on heat from their surroundings or, more often, direct from the sun's rays. In Britain, reptiles are dormant in winter because they cannot reach their working temperatures. In spring they emerge on sunny days, but the sunshine is so weak they need to bask almost all the time. As the sun gets stronger, basking time is shorter – mainly early and late in the day – and there is time for hunting and breeding. By midsummer basking is hardly necessary, but as autumn comes the need increases, and finally the animals are forced into hibernation.

5 *Heaps of stable manure or rotting plants generate heat, which makes them suitable basking spots for grass snakes.*

FIELDCRAFT

Rejected ragwort
A field with a lot of ragwort has probably been grazed by horses. Both horses and cows find ragwort distasteful but a horse can be more selective in its eating. It bites off plants between its teeth, whereas a cow pulls them up in clumps by curling its tongue round them.

A fox's leavings
The hind-leg bones and the foot of a rabbit are likely to be the remains of a fox's meal, and often have a distinctive, musky fox scent. They may have been dropped by a fox or, if the bones are picked clean, by a scavenging crow.

A fox's droppings
Fragments of bone, matted fur and seeds are contained in the droppings of a fox; the droppings have a characteristic twisted tail.

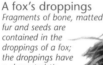

Tracks and signs in downland and pasture

MOST WILD ANIMALS stay under cover in daylight, venturing out only after dark. So you are likely to see few during the day in open fields and downland. To a keen eye, though, there are usually plenty of signs that reveal the presence of numerous species. The signs described here are typical of the type of country shown, but are not the only ones that may be found there.

Because fields and grassland are frequently grazed by farm animals, the footprints, droppings and hairs of wild animals can easily be confused with those of domestic species. Sheep and deer, for instance, both have cloven

hoofs, and it is difficult to distinguish between their tracks. Generally, deer tracks in a particular spot are fewer in number than those of sheep, as sheep live in large groups. Deer are surprisingly common, even in well-inhabited countryside, although they usually stay hidden from sight. Red, sika, fallow and roe deer are the species whose tracks are most likely to be confused with those of sheep. Pastureland where sheep graze is usually close-cropped and unlikely to support many small mammals, except around field edges, where hedgerows and longer grass afford food and shelter.

Where to look for footprints
A small patch of mud, often found near a gate or on a rutted path, is a good place to look for animal tracks. The cloven hoof-prints of sheep and deer are difficult to tell apart, but there may be other identifying signs nearby, such as wool or hair.

Hind   *Fore*

A badger's fore and hind feet can be mistaken for the tracks of two different animals.

A dog's pawprints are broad and often have the front toes splayed.

A fox's tracks are narrow, with the front toes close together.

Sheep tracks have one half of the hoof larger than the other.

Deer tracks have both halves of the hoof the same size but often more widely separated.

Trampled trails in the grass
Beaten tracks in the grass that look like footpaths may be animal trails. If they pass under fences or low bushes and shrubs, they have been made by an animal. Footpaths made by humans go over or round such obstacles, or trample them down.

Sheep trails are usually narrow. They often cut deep into soft ground and expose the bare earth.

Badger paths are usually well-worn tracks about 15cm wide. Normally the grass is flattened, but no earth is exposed.

How to recognise hairs

Where animal trails pass under a chain-link or barbed-wire fence, hair can be scraped off an animal's back. Hairs caught on the top strand of a fence are likely to be from horses or cattle, which rub their necks along it, or from deer that have leapt over it. Small deer also squeeze under fences.

Tell-tale wisps

Where sheep have grazed, pieces of greyish-white fleece often get caught on brambles and thistles.

Badger hairs are wiry and 50-75mm long. They are white, with a black zone near the tapered end.

Cattle hairs are fairly short and soft, and mat together like felt.

Deer hairs are stiff, straight and bristly.

Rabbit hairs are fine, soft and fluffy. They are about 13mm long, and grey with a fawn tip.

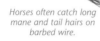

Top wire

Horses often catch long mane and tail hairs on barbed wire.

Bottom wire

Fox hairs are about 25mm long. They are straight and red-brown or grey-brown with a pale tip.

Honey for the badger

Common wasps and some wild bees make nests underground in holes or burrows, often in a bank. A dug-up bees' nest is the work of a badger, which eats the larvae and stored honey. Its shaggy coat protects it from stings.

Bottles as deathtraps

*Small mammals go into bottles to look for food or simply to explore. They are often **unable to get out again**, so die of starvation and cold. Thousands are trapped in this way every year, and up to 28 have been found in one bottle. Discarded bottles with animal remains are most likely to be found in lay-bys. Where only the skeletons are left, the skulls can be used to identify the trapped animals.*

A shrew skull (above and right) is narrow and pointed and does not have prominent cheek bones. The teeth are tipped with red and are continuous along the jaw.

A mouse (or rat) jaw has knobbly molar teeth; if the teeth are removed, each leaves several tiny root holes.

A rodent skull (above and right) such as that of a vole or mouse has prominent cheek bones and eye sockets, and there is a gap between the incisor teeth at the front and the molar teeth at the back.

A vole jaw has a zigzag pattern on the grinding surface of its molars; if the teeth are removed, each leaves one big, ragged hole.

Animal tracks and traces in road lay-bys

LAY-BYS ARE OFTEN untidy places, and the rubbish that people leave there is all too evident in winter when the blanket of green vegetation dies back. To the local mammals, the rubbish can be a blessing or a disaster. Picnic remains and other food may be welcome to a hungry animal, particularly in frosty weather when natural food is hard to find. Unsightly junk may also provide a cosy and weatherproof nest site.

But discarded bottles and drink cans are often death traps for the small mammals that venture into them. More than 50 mice, voles and shrews may die in bottles in a single lay-by in the space of a few months, and up to five different species may be trapped in one milk bottle. Their corpses provide a feast for flies and carrion beetles but are a health hazard for humans, as well as a sad reminder of the suffering caused by people too thoughtless to take their rubbish home. Larger animals are also at risk from litter. A hedgehog can get its snout stuck in opened bean or soup cans and plastic cartons. Deer and sheep step on rusty tins and pick up an uncomfortable anklet that may cause septic wounds. Many animals, including dogs, risk dangerous cuts to feet and noses from broken glass and jagged metal.

Wayside warehouses

An old bullfinch or blackbird nest containing chewed hawthorn berries or rose hips may have been used as a feeding place by a wood mouse. Small mammals such as mice and voles sometimes climb into bushes to feed on fruit.

A cardboard canopy

Large pieces of rubbish – corrugated iron sheets or cardboard boxes, for example – provide shelter for field voles, whose well-worn runway systems can often be found underneath. There may also be a nest made from finely chewed plants.

Vigour from decay

The rotted remains of litter add nitrogen to the soil. The result is flourishing clumps of elder bushes and nettles, which like rich soil.

Cans that kill

Like bottles, drink cans are traps for small animals. But because the entrance hole is so small, they usually catch only shrews, which are tiny with a narrow head.

Elder flower and berries

Nettles

Homes in hedgerows and banks

Litter in lay-bys is a source of extra food for mammals in winter. Where there is also a hedgerow with plenty of cover, several kinds of burrowing mammals may live in a lay-by.

A rabbit hole (above) is normally about 75mm across. There are usually several near each other, with a lot of bare earth around. There are also small, dry, spherical droppings.

The hole of a brown rat (above) is about 40mm across, usually with a narrow, beaten trail leading to it. Sometimes there are a few oval droppings nearby.

A badger hole (left) is about 30cm wide and is generally in a slope on light, well-drained soil. Usually, the hole does not smell and has no food remains outside; there may be loose soil containing badger hairs, thrown out with discarded nesting material.

A fox hole (right) is about 25cm across, with a long mound of excavated soil – and sometimes food remains such as bones outside. Often there is a strong smell of fox in the vicinity of the hole.

Footprints in focus

The soft, slimy mud at the water's edge shows fine detail of even small footprints such as those of water voles, the ones most likely to be seen. They can be confused with the prints of the brown rat, also seen near water. Mole footprints may be seen in wet meadows, after flood water has forced them to leave their burrows.

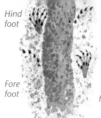

Hind foot

Fore foot

A mole (left) tends to walk on the inner side of its fore feet, so its fore prints show only the marks of its five claw tips, not the rest of its foot. Its legs are short, so its belly makes a drag mark.

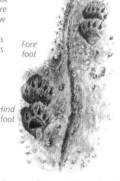

Fore foot

Hind foot

Otter tracks, up to 60mm long and as wide as they are long, show five-toed webbed feet. Drag marks made by the animal's tail can often be seen.

A brown rat (below) has four toes on its fore feet and five toes on its larger hind feet, but its prints are slightly larger than a water vole's. The rat's hind feet are 35mm long, or more.

Fore foot

Hind foot

A water vole (above) does not have webbed feet. There are four toes on its fore feet and five toes on its larger hind feet. The hind feet are up to 25mm long.

Fore foot

Hind foot

Tracks and signs by the waterside

THE MUDDY BANK of a river or stream shows up animal footprints particularly well. So does the soft, moist soil of a wet riverside meadow that floods in winter when low evaporation rates and heavy rain make water levels rise. The softer the mud, the finer the detail of the prints.

Footprints in a field are not always perfect. Sometimes only the claws or toes mark the soil, especially on dry ground, with no print from the palm or sole of the foot. The fore feet of water voles and rats, for instance, often leave only sets of four small toe marks in an arc. Where several animals have crossed the ground, or one has moved over the same area repeatedly, a mass of confusing, overlapping prints is likely. But there may be clues nearby to the animal's identity, such as food debris or droppings. As well as animals that live beside the water, look for the tracks of animals that drink at the water's edge, such as badgers, foxes and deer. Bird footprints – look for the long middle toe – can be plentiful, especially those of ducks, herons and moorhens.

Burrows at the water's edge
Burrows may be found where there are low banks of soft earth by slow-flowing rivers. Water vole burrows and perhaps a kingfisher's nest hole are the commonest.

The entrance to a water vole burrow is a hole about 50mm across. It is in a waterside bank at or near water level.

A kingfisher's nest hole is similar in size to a water vole burrow but is at least 60cm above water level, and normally in a bare, vertical bank.

Territory markers
The droppings of aquatic mammals such as mink and otter may be found on a fallen tree or boulder at the water's edge. The animals leave droppings as scent markers to define territory. Tracks in the mud nearby help identification.

Untidy voles
Chewed plant fragments, bitten-off stems and shreds of pith signify the presence of water voles, which feed on sedges and other waterside plants. Look out for tracks, droppings and also burrow entrances nearby.

Otter droppings (spraints) are dark and slimy with a strong, somewhat fishy smell. Fish scales and bone fragments may be visible.

Mink droppings are smaller than otter spraints, but may also contain scales and bones. They are foul-smelling and when fresh are dark green.

Geese among the mammals
Canada goose droppings – large, soft and green and white – are often seen in heaps beside water. Mammal droppings differ in having no white in them, nor are they as long and thin as the goose droppings.

Water vole tracks are usually in groups around plant fragments, overlapping each other. There may be wet, shiny patches where water has run off the fur.

Water vole droppings are oval and about 13mm long. They are dark green or brown, usually in groups of about half a dozen, with vole prints all round them.

An ever-ready larder
In mixed woods, squirrels often choose to live in conifers such as Scots pines, which provide them with year-round food and shelter. Look for chewed cones scattered beneath pines or other conifers.

A squirrel (red or grey) bites the scales off a ripe cone to get at the seeds inside. Chewed cores and neatly bitten-off scales are dropped.

Crossbills also drop discarded pine or spruce cones below trees. Usually the scales are not torn off but prised open with the beak and split.

Hedgehog sign
Hedgehog droppings are sometimes seen on pathways. They are usually single, black, crinkly, about 40mm long and often studded with the remnants of chewed beetles.

Tracks in the mud
A muddy wheel rut in a woodland ride (see opposite) is a good place to look for animal tracks, particularly those of deer. Look, too, at the edge of a ditch where animals jump across.

Fallow deer hoofprints are roughly 64mm long and about 40mm across.

When deer jump and land in soft mud, their hoofprints are widely splayed and the dew claws are often imprinted.

Dew claws

Red deer hoofprints are roughly 80mm long and 64mm across.

Roe deer hoofprints are roughly 45mm long and 35mm across.

Muntjac hoofprints are less than 30mm long and 25mm across.

Tracks and signs in mixed woodland

MIXED WOODLAND often provides shelter for more different kinds of animals than any other type of country, but it takes patience and a keen eye to find their signs. Tracks and trails do not show up well in leaf litter, and in autumn are soon hidden by falling leaves. But there are often animal footprints in the muddy rides and bare patches of soil, although it is rarely possible to follow a trail far before it becomes lost in the undergrowth. There are also animal signs such as hairs, droppings and food remains to be seen, although they are not easy to pick out amid the entanglement of trees and bushes.

On dry woodland soils, paw tracks – especially dog tracks – do not show the whole print, only the two front toes, and could be mistaken for the cloven hoofprints of deer. Usually the distinct claw marks to be seen at

Old bones for new
Antlers lying on the ground after being cast by deer are often gnawed by rodents, as they are a source of calcium, which helps to strengthen bones.

Nests in coppice stools
Trees are coppiced by being cut off near the ground. This encourages the growth of clusters of slim, straight shoots for use as poles. Stumps (stools) accumulate a mass of dry, dead leaves that are ideal places for dormice to hibernate in winter. Several other species, such as wood mice, may nest there too.

the tips of the toes of pawprints help to avoid confusion. The droppings of different species have distinctive shapes, but the colour and texture depend very much on what the animal has been eating, which often varies according to the time of year. Generally, groups of smooth, uniform pellets are those of plant eaters, and ragged pellets found singly or two or three together are those of carnivores.

Saplings spoiled by deer
In April roe bucks fray the bark of saplings such as birches when they rub off velvet from their new antlers. The ground below is churned up by their hoofs. They also rub scent on saplings from April into July.

Thickets that shelter deer

Deer often shelter beside a windproof holly thicket or dense coppice, or under yew trees. Piles of droppings (fewmets) accumulate there.

Fallow deer droppings are black and cylindrical with a small point at one end. They are roughly 16mm long and usually in clusters.

Red deer droppings are black and cylindrical with a small point at one end. They are up to 25mm long and usually in clusters.

Muntjac droppings are black and less than 10mm long. They are round or slightly elongated and usually in clusters.

Roe deer droppings are oval and roughly 10-15mm long. They are usually in clusters and may be black or brown.

Hazel tree harvest

Hazel nuts from woodland and hedgerow trees are a major food for rodents, which gnaw them in different ways depending on the species. Study the discarded remains of nuts to identify the eater. You may need a lens to see the toothmarks.

A dormouse gnaws a hole in the side of the nut and then enlarges it by turning the nut round and scooping the edge with its teeth. This leaves toothmarks on the cut edge but few on the nut surface.

A bank vole gnaws a hole with a regular, clean-cut edge. It leaves few if any toothmarks on the nut surface.

A wood mouse gnaws a neat hole with an irregular, chamfered edge. There are traces of toothmarks on the nut's shiny surface.

A squirrel's jaws can shatter a nut in the same way as nutcrackers can. It leaves fragments of irregular shape with jagged edges and no obvious toothmarks.

Signs that aid identification

When attempting to recognise animal tracks, look for other identifying clues, such as droppings.

Fore

Hind

Squirrel tracks

A rabbit trail may be identified because it leads from a burrow. Often there are heaps of droppings nearby.

Tracks coming down from a tree are most likely those of a squirrel. Squirrels come out on fine days in winter, even in snow, and usually move in a series of bounds. The tracks appear in groups of four about 50cm apart.

Reading the stories in the snow

A LAYER OF SNOW will show up the tracks of all kinds of animals not normally seen and whose presence was unsuspected. In snow, no animal can move anywhere without leaving footprints, so snow provides a great opportunity to gain information about the movements and habits of wild creatures. Light snow, or even heavy frost, shows up individual tracks. Thicker snow that blankets the ground often allows trails to be followed for considerable distances. In really deep snow few trails are likely; it is so difficult to walk in that not many animals venture out.

Generally, only the tracks of fairly big animals – squirrels and larger creatures – are found in snow. Smaller animals such as mice and voles stay under the snow blanket because their food is there, and it is warmer and more protected from icy winds. Trails in the snow often lead to where an animal has fed – a rabbit scraping through to find grass, for example. With the trail of a predator there may also be tracks of the prey, as well as its remains. Other signs of an animal, such as droppings or urine stains in the snow, may also be found near its tracks.

How speed affects trails
The pattern of an animal's footprints varies according to its gait – hopping, trotting or galloping, for example.

A trotting fallow deer places its hind feet just in front of the prints of its fore feet, producing a staggered trail of partly overlapping prints, all more or less evenly spaced. When galloping, it puts its hind feet well in front of its fore feet. Its prints are in fours, separated by longish gaps. Often prints are splayed and the marks of dew claws show.

Different ways of walking revealed
Trails in the snow usually have a whole succession of footprints, and so give a good opportunity to study the different ways in which animals walk.

A fox trail is almost a single line because a fox puts its hind feet into the prints of its fore feet and draws in its feet below the mid line of its body.

A dog trail has prints staggered to each side of its body line, being relatively wider-bodied and shorter-legged than a fox. It does not put its hind feet exactly into the prints of its fore feet.

Hind foot (about 90mm)

Fore foot

Hind foot

A badger walks with its feet pointing inwards; the hind prints often overlap the rear of the fore prints. Often the prints are muddy from soil on the feet. Badgers do not hibernate; trails may be seen between sett entrances.

A rabbit moving slowly hops along. The prints of its hind feet are just behind the prints of its fore feet. But when it moves fast, it bounds in much longer strides. Its hind footprints appear in front of its fore footprints.

Trotting

Galloping

Hopping

Bounding

How size and speed alter stride
As an animal's gait gets faster, the length of its stride increases, indicated by the distance between sets of prints. This also indicates an animal's size. Different kinds of deer, for example, all moving at the same gait, can be identified by stride.

Trotting red deer

Distance between prints 76cm

Trotting fallow deer

Distance between prints about 50cm

Trotting roe deer

Distance between prints about 45cm

Look-alike tracks and trails
Some animal tracks are very similar and need careful study to observe differences such as shape.

Dog   *Fox*

The tracks of a small dog and a fox are similar. But the dog's tracks are broader and more splayed, and the fox's tracks have the two middle toes closer together than the dog's.

Distorted tracks in melted snow
Footprints discovered as a thaw begins can be misleading, as they become enlarged and distorted.

Cat in fresh snow

Cat in melting snow

THE HIND LEG OF A DEER

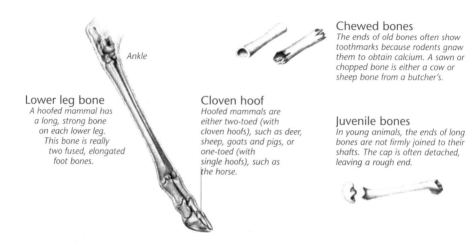

Ankle

Lower leg bone
A hoofed mammal has a long, strong bone on each lower leg. This bone is really two fused, elongated foot bones.

Cloven hoof
Hoofed mammals are either two-toed (with cloven hoofs), such as deer, sheep, goats and pigs, or one-toed (with single hoofs), such as the horse.

Chewed bones
The ends of old bones often show toothmarks because rodents gnaw them to obtain calcium. A sawn or chopped bone is either a cow or sheep bone from a butcher's.

Juvenile bones
In young animals, the ends of long bones are not firmly joined to their shafts. The cap is often detached, leaving a rough end.

How to identify bones

IT IS NOT UNUSUAL to find animal bones, or even whole skeletons. Dead animals, especially larger ones, are rarely eaten whole by predators or scavengers because their bones are too big and indigestible. Bones are often carried off and left elsewhere. Even mice will drag small bones away to gnaw them for their calcium content, and the bones of animals that died underground are often dug up and scattered during later burrowing activities.

All land mammals have a similar bone structure, and by studying the size and shape of bones and skulls it is possible to get an idea of the part they played in the animal's make-up, and perhaps to identify the animal they came from.

Bones can be a health risk unless well weathered and cleaned of flesh. Handle them with a stick, or protect your hands with a polythene bag or rubber gloves.

THE SKELETON OF A RABBIT

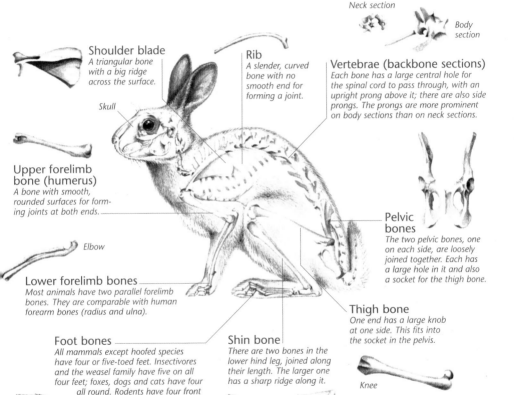

Neck section

Body section

Shoulder blade
A triangular bone with a big ridge across the surface.

Skull

Rib
A slender, curved bone with no smooth end for forming a joint.

Vertebrae (backbone sections)
Each bone has a large central hole for the spinal cord to pass through, with an upright prong above it; there are also side prongs. The prongs are more prominent on body sections than on neck sections.

Upper forelimb bone (humerus)
A bone with smooth, rounded surfaces for forming joints at both ends.

Elbow

Pelvic bones
The two pelvic bones, one on each side, are loosely joined together. Each has a large hole in it and also a socket for the thigh bone.

Lower forelimb bones
Most animals have two parallel forelimb bones. They are comparable with human forearm bones (radius and ulna).

Foot bones
All mammals except hoofed species have four or five-toed feet. Insectivores and the weasel family have five on all four feet; foxes, dogs and cats have four all round. Rodents have four front toes and five hind toes, rabbits and hares the reverse.

Shin bone
There are two bones in the lower hind leg, joined along their length. The larger one has a sharp ridge along it.

Thigh bone
One end has a large knob at one side. This fits into the socket in the pelvis.

Knee

Hoofed mammals

Hoofed mammals are plant eaters, so normally have no canine teeth for seizing prey. There is a big gap between the incisors (used for cutting) at the front of the jaw and the molars (used for grinding) towards the rear. Horses and pigs have incisors on both upper and lower jaws. Other hoofed mammals have a toothless pad at the front of the upper jaw.

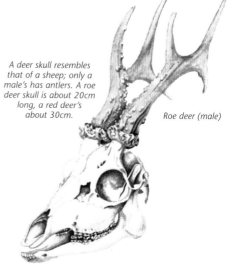

A deer skull resembles that of a sheep; only a male's has antlers. A roe deer skull is about 20cm long, a red deer's about 30cm.

Roe deer (male)

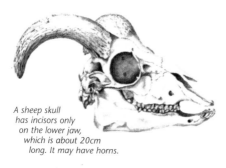

A sheep skull has incisors only on the lower jaw, which is about 20cm long. It may have horns.

Recognising skulls

THE MAIN WAYS of identifying a skull are by its size and by the type and arrangement of the teeth. Complete skulls of larger animals are often found. Those of small mammals such as mice, voles and shrews are under 25mm long and are most unlikely to be discovered except in discarded bottles (the remains of trapped animals, see page 237) or owl pellets.

Hares and rabbits

The skull of a rabbit or hare is similar to a rodent's skull but has a second pair of tiny incisors behind the grooved front pair in the upper jaw. The molar teeth have an oval surface.

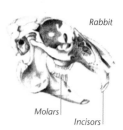

Rabbit

Molars

Incisors

A rabbit's skull is up to 85mm long. An adult hare's is longer.

Carnivores

The skulls of carnivores such as foxes and cats, which are flesh eaters, have teeth all the way along the jaw. They have large, sharp-pointed canine teeth towards the front.

Rodents

The skull of a rodent such as a rat or squirrel has a big gap between the incisors at the front of the jaws and the molars towards the rear. Rodent incisors have a yellow or orange front surface not found in other mammals. Rats, like mice, have molars with a knobbly surface.

A badger skull is about 12.5cm long. It is broader than a fox skull and has big, flat-topped molars. Its lower jaw will not detach from its upper jaw.

A fox skull is about 12.5cm long. Mink, polecat, stoat and weasel skulls are less than 64mm long.

A red squirrel skull is about 54mm long at the most. A grey squirrel skull is about 60mm long.

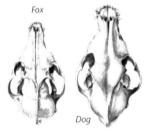

Fox

Dog

Insectivores

Like carnivores, insectivores such as shrews and hedgehogs have teeth all along the jaw, with no big gaps between incisors and molars. But unlike carnivores, they do not have big canines. Their teeth have very sharp points.

A cat skull is rounded, with short jaws, and is about 75mm long. All the teeth are pointed.

Viewed from above, a fox skull can be distinguished from a dog skull by the eyebrow ridges. In a fox they have concave pits, in a dog they are convex, giving bulging brows.

A hedgehog skull is about 50mm long. Two almost horizontal lower front incisors fit into a gap between the two prominent upper incisors.

INDEX

Page numbers in bold type refer to the main entry.

Wild Britain: Animals is based on material in *Reader's Digest Nature Lover's Library: Field Guide to the Animals of Britain* published by The Reader's Digest Association Limited, London.

First Edition Copyright © 2008
The Reader's Digest Association Limited,
11 Westferry Circus, Canary Wharf,
London E14 4HE
www.readersdigest.co.uk

Origination by Colour Systems Limited, London
Printed in China

We are committed both to the quality of our products and the service we provide to our customers. We value your comments, so please do contact us on **08705 113366** or via our website at
www.readersdigest.co.uk

If you have any comments or suggestions about the content of our books, email us at
gbeditorial@readersdigest.co.uk

Book code 400-375 UP0000-1
ISBN 978 0 276 44272 8
Oracle code 250011836H.00.24

Acknowledgments

COVER f and **b** ardea.com/Rolf Kopfle; 2–3 ShutterStock, Inc/Vladimir Chernyanskiy; 32-33 naturepl.com/Nick Garbutt; 232-3 ShutterStock, Inc/Markabond
MAPS Jenny Doodge
ILLUSTRATIONS Peter Barrett; Jim Channell; Kevin Dean; Brian Delf; Sarah Fox-Davies; John Francis; Rosalind Hewitt; H. Jacob; Robert Morton; David Nockels; Eric Robson; Gill Tomblin; Libby Turner; Phil Weare

EDITORS John Andrews, Lisa Thomas
ART EDITOR Austin Taylor
EDITORIAL CONSULTANT John Woodward
PROOFREADER Barry Gage
INDEXER Marie Lorimer

Reader's Digest General Books
EDITORIAL DIRECTOR Julian Browne
ART DIRECTOR Anne-Marie Bulat
MANAGING EDITOR Nina Hathway
HEAD OF BOOK DEVELOPMENT Sarah Bloxham
PICTURE RESOURCE MANAGER
Sarah Stewart-Richardson
PRE-PRESS ACCOUNT MANAGER Dean Russell
PRODUCTION CONTROLLER
Katherine Bunn
PRODUCT PRODUCTION MANAGER
Claudette Bramble